WONDER
and Other Life Skills

WONDER
and Other Life Skills

**Spiritual Life
Retreats**
for
Young Adults
Using the
Creative Arts

B. Kathleen Fannin

COWLEY PUBLICATIONS
Lanham, Chicago, New York, Toronto, and Plymouth, UK

Published by Cowley Publications
An imprint of Rowman & Littlefield Publishers, Inc.
A wholly owned subsidary of The Rowman & Littlefield Publishing
Group, Inc.
4501 Forbes Boulevard, Suite 200
Lanham, MD 20706

Estover Road
Plymouth PL6 7PY
United Kingdom

Distributed by National Book Network

Library of Congress Cataloging-in-Publication Data

Fannin, B. Kathleen.
     Wonder and other life skills : spiritual life retreats for young adults
using the creative arts / B. Kathleen Fannin.
          p. cm.
     Includes index.
     ISBN-13: 978-1-56101-307-4 (pbk. : alk. paper)
     ISBN-10: 1-56101-307-2 (pbk. : alk. paper)
     1. Church work with youth. 2. Church work with young adults.
     3. Spiritual retreats. I. Title.
     BV4447.F36 2007
     269'.634—dc22   2007015260

Printed in the United States of America.

♾™ The paper used in this publication meets the minimum requirements
of American National Standard for Information Sciences—Permanence of
Paper for Printed Library Materials, ANSI/NISO Z39.48-1992.

Contents

Introduction

Human beings are spiritual creatures. As Dr. Gerald May notes, we have a fundamental spiritual longing with "... three basic dimensions: a desire for unconditional love, a need for belonging and union, [and] a deep hunger to 'just be.'"[1] This longing is exacerbated by the high value placed on individualism, self-determination, and productivity in U.S. culture. I believe, at least in this country, that as we enter the twenty-first century, the hectic pace of our technocratic, media-inundated existence has left many of us bereft of spiritual nurture and a sense of community.

The resulting hunger is prevalent throughout our society, expressed as an emptiness or longing by people who worship in various Christian denominations and other faiths, as well as by folks who have "given up" on organized religion altogether. As Dr. Bruce Epperly noted in a class on the "Spirituality of Campus Ministry" we are "ecstasy deprived."[2] I am convinced that a lack of meaningful spiritual nurture prior to students' arrival on college campuses lies at the root of a general apathy toward participation in campus religious life. This lack is also reflected in abuse of alcohol and drugs, eating disorders, and many other self-destructive behaviors that manifest themselves among the students I serve as a college chaplain.[3] I find it more than mere coincidence

that one of the more potent and popular illicit drugs is called
"ecstasy."

How can college chaplains, campus ministers, and local pas-
tors help students overcome their apathy? How can we turn them
on to the community-building, life-giving, life-enduring ecstasy of
spiritual experience and offer them a sense of belonging that will
help them develop moral virtues to turn them away from the iso-
lating, life-threatening, temporary ecstasies of drugs, alcohol, com-
puter games, meaningless and demeaning sexual encounters, etc.?
These are questions that illuminate symptoms of the larger problem many students face: low self-esteem. Henri Nouwen notes,
"self-rejection is the greatest enemy of the spiritual life because it
contradicts the sacred voice that calls us the beloved."[4]

From the time they set foot on campus, college students have
their attention pulled in many directions as they sort out issues of
leaving home, living with a roommate, wanting to fit in, finding
time to study, choosing cocurricular activities, encountering people of other cultures and faith traditions, and sorting out their own
spiritual identities. Most students at the college where I serve as the
Chaplain fall into the eighteen to twenty-three age bracket, a time
in their lives when ambiguity is very unsettling, issues of belonging
and meaning are paramount, and spiritual hunger is deep. I have
developed a series of retreats as tools to help ministers who work
with college-aged young adults offer spiritual nurture to this often
hard-to-reach population. These retreats employ creative arts (e.g.,
collage, painting, poetry writing, mandalas) and spiritual disciplines
(e.g., prayer, silence, journaling, mindfulness, guided meditation)
as ways of opening students' minds to ingenuity, innovation, and
imagination to help them connect with the Divine. These retreats
would also be helpful resources for the larger Church as it endeavors to nurture the spiritual lives of young adults. Additionally, they
are a tool churches could use to create intergenerational experiences for members of their congregations.

It is apparent that one of the paradigms that rules the lives of
college students today is "Success!" Valuing success, we focus on
productivity and undervalue activities which have no immediately
discernable product—such as being still, engaging in daily spiritual
practice, enjoying a sunset, or pondering the big questions[5] that

lead to a greater sense of belonging, self-worth, and ethical values. Intuition that fosters the creative arts and leads to deeper ways of knowing is held in low esteem.[6] In the midst of life's many demands, finding time for God can be difficult. Often participation in spiritual life programming is the first thing students drop as deadlines for papers loom and midterm or final exams draw near.

Yet the message of the gospel is a message of taking time away from our daily hustle and hurry just to *be*, with one another and with God.[7] Being in relationship, with each other and with the Divine, is the primary purpose of being human, a purpose directly at odds with one of our primary cultural values, self-absorbed individualism, the me-first, winner-take-all, pull-yourself-up-by-your-own-bootstraps sort of machismo[8] that has developed in American culture from the early days of the American Frontier (early 1800s) onward. It is an individualism that is so self-centered as to have a total disregard for the well-being of others and which is prepared to do whatever it takes to get ahead.

Perhaps religious teachings about the importance for one's own well-being of community and loving one's neighbor could help combat this alarming social paradigm, but students (and others) shy away from organized religion. I believe one reason is that whatever experience they may have had growing up resulted in what Marcus Borg calls "secondhand religion . . . a way of being religious based on believing what one has heard from others" rather than "firsthand religion" through which one develops a personal relationship "to that which the Bible and the teachings of the church point—namely, that reality we call God or the Spirit of God."[9]

Martin Buber published *Ich and Du*[10] in 1922. In this work he discussed two distinct ways for persons to be in the world. The "I-It" mode is how we make sense of our ordinary experience. This is "the world of cause and effect, of ordered space and time; the world as domesticated by the culturally created grid of language, categories, and knowledge."[11] This is the world of objective knowing. Buber describes the other way of being in the world as "I-You." This is "the world of relation and connectedness as opposed to separation and differentiation."[12] I believe popular culture has become focused on the "I-It" mode, teaching our children that other persons are "Its" to be used for self-promotion.

The voices of parents and educators (including religious leaders) that speak to the value of relationships over the accumulation of wealth and self-aggrandizement get drowned out by the blitz of cultural messages that equate success with personal wealth, to be attained at any cost. Sadly, some parents encourage their children to attend college, not in order to achieve an education but to improve their chances for obtaining a "good" job (i.e., a job that pays well).

In the chapters that follow, we shall explore our need for community in order to be fully human, our need for moral virtues in order to develop and maintain relationships with God and with each other, the necessity of community for the development of moral virtues, ways in which community might be created in a multifaith environment, the implications of humans being created in the image of God, and the ramifications of God's apparent desire to be in relationship with humankind. Following these explorations, I shall discuss in detail two of the retreat experiences I have had with my students at Monmouth College in Monmouth, Illinois. In chapter 7 the reader will find outlines for six additional retreats which can be adapted to particular time frames, specific retreat settings, and other idiosyncratic demands of environments in which ministry for young adults may be offered. Chapter 8 provides detailed instructions for carrying out various creative arts and other retreat activities. Finally, in chapter 9 the reader will find the insights and understandings I gained from retreat experiences with my students as well as my recommendations for offering retreats for college students and/or for other small groups or entire congregations in local churches.

ONE

Our Need for a New Paradigm
Self-Absorbed Individualism vs. Community in an Age of Moral Ambiguity

I f the purpose of being human is to be in relationship with other humans and with God, if community is necessary to shape the moral virtues required for humans to achieve this primary purpose, and if moral virtues are necessary to maintain community, then self-absorbed individualism, culturally instilled, transmitted, and valued, is detrimental to human moral formation and to our subsequent ability and desire to fulfill the primary purpose of being human. In this chapter I shall argue that the primary purpose of being human is, indeed, to be in relationship with other humans and with God. Additionally, I shall explore the ideas that community is necessary for moral formation and that without moral virtues humans cannot maintain community. I agree with Scott Peck who believes "the reality is that we are inevitably social creatures who desperately need each other not merely for sustenance, not merely for company, but for any meaning to our lives whatsoever."[1] Yet, as necessary as community is to human well-being and fulfillment of the primary purpose of being human, I maintain that American culture promotes a morality of self-centered, self-absorbed individualism which directly opposes community formation.

Human and Divine Mutuality and Vulnerability

Being in relationship with others requires a certain amount of vulnerability. It requires risking an openness with one another that brings the possibility that we can be hurt. Lee Bolman and Terrance Deal suggest that vulnerability requires "a willingness to reach out and open one's heart. An open heart is vulnerable. Confronting vulnerability allows us to drop our mask, meet heart to heart and be present for one another."[2] But vulnerability is antithetical to our cultural paradigm of self-sufficient individualism and has no moral value in a world where ultimate weapons can bring total annihilation at the press of a button.[3]

The openness and mutuality required for relationship demands vulnerability from both parties in the relationship. If only one is vulnerable and open, then the other becomes at best a benign ruler, and at worst an abuser. Relationship requires the mutuality that only results when both parties are open with one another and risk the possibility of being wounded in order to give and receive love.

The scriptures of many traditions, including Christianity, tell us we are to love one another and God as God loves us (John 15:12). We proclaim that God does indeed love us (though sadly, many churches engage in Christian exclusivism, proclaiming God loves only Christians, thus making it godly to hate one's non-Christian neighbor[4]). We profess our love for God. But while we claim such communion with God, we often fail to grasp the mutual vulnerability this implies. Stephen Post asserts that "mutual love or reciprocity is the only appropriate fundamental norm for human interrelations and for the Divine-human encounter as well."[5]

But in American culture God is often imaged as all-powerful and judgmental, an image that is directly in conflict with the concept of Divine vulnerability and certainly one that interferes with the development of mutual relationship. Young adults who were taught as children that God is judgmental and wrathful find it difficult to maintain a meaningful relationship with God. Only when we can heal that image of God can we also discover a new understanding of ourselves in relationship to the Divine.[6] As long as we are convinced that God is about power and judgment and has no need for our love except as it proves our obedience to Divine rule, we will continue to view vulnerability as ungodly.

That being the case, we who are made in God's image had better avoid vulnerability too. This compels us to hide the wounds that all of us have. Yet it is only through sharing "our brokenness, defeats, failures, doubts, inadequacies, and sins"[7] that we can ever hope to achieve the communion of relationship—with one another and with God. As William Placher suggest, "if we Christians understand the doctrine of the Trinity right, we will realize that it implies that God is not about power and self-sufficiency, and the assertion of authority but about mutuality and equality and love."[8]

In American society, I believe invulnerability has become a cultural idol that requires us to deny that we are not perfect, we do have weaknesses, and we need each other. Scott Peck notes that

> this denial can be sustained only by pretense. Because we cannot ever be totally adequate, self-sufficient, independent beings, the ideal of rugged individualism encourages us to fake it. It encourages us to hide our weaknesses and failures. It teaches us to be utterly ashamed of our limitations. It drives us to attempt to be superwomen and supermen not only in the eyes of others but also in our own. It pushes us day in and day out to look as if we "had it all together," as if we were without needs and in total control of our lives. It also relentlessly isolates us from each other. And it makes genuine community impossible.[9]

Mere individualism, as such, is not the problem. We need to differentiate ourselves from one another in order to know who we are. The psychological process of individuation[10] is critical to our functioning within the human community. "Authentic interpersonal communion presupposes the full realization of the individual persons who enter into it."[11] Self-realization is the precondition of self-giving.[12]

Each of us is a unique individual. But our culture has equated *individualism* with *freedom from the need for others*. What I am calling *self-absorbed individualism* is a sense of competitive autonomy without a context of moral or religious obligation. It is a sort of "rugged individualism" that implies freedom without responsibility. It is an individualism "in which the self has become the main form of reality with no relation to a larger whole"[13] and in which everything in a person's world revolves around the fostering, acclamation, and gratification of the self.[14] It is self-centered, self-sufficient, self-absorbed individualism as opposed to individuality and, as noted above, it makes genuine community impossible. Furthermore, if "morality requires interpersonal consideration, whereby each person must be concerned for the important interests of other persons besides himself or herself,"[15] then holding this sort of culturally defined individualism as an ideal interferes with one's moral formation.

Morality Is a Communal Concept

Though I believe one can certainly be moral or immoral outside the context of a particular community, I do not believe one can develop moral virtues alone any more than one can sort out one's personal identity in a vacuum. It has been nearly twenty years since Robert Bellah wrote that "we find ourselves not independently of other people and institutions but through them. We never get to the bottom of ourselves on our own. We discover who we are face to face and side by side with others in work, love, and learning."[16] We need other people to reflect back to us concepts of the self we are trying to discover. This is the process of individuation that leads us to "the positive aspects of individuality: the dignity, worth, and moral autonomy of the individual."[17] We cannot discern a self alone, nor can we develop a morality except in relation to other human beings.

Additionally, we cannot develop moral concepts without a language to conceptualize them. "Moral sentiments would not be possible without the higher mental powers and abstract concepts made possible by language and community."[18] But Alasdair MacIntyre suggests that modern society has lost the context in which the moral language we use was developed, making it difficult, if not impossible, for us to agree on what the language means. As a society, we lack the agreements that at one time undergirded social morality.[19]

In ancient heroic societies every citizen had a specifically defined role that contributed to the success of the city-state. Morality and one's social status were one and the same thing; correct behavior was defined as that which was in accordance with one's social role. If one engaged in actions that caused one to fall short of one's social role, one fell short of what morality dictated. In such a society, "virtues are those qualities which sustain a free man [sic] in his role and which manifest themselves in those actions which the role requires."[20] Furthermore, the self could only be understood in terms of one's social role. There was no such thing as an individual outside the social context.[21] The Greek city-state had an idea of what a person is, what human life is aimed at, what human flourishing is, and what success and human excellence look like. There was a set of assumptions that made the conversation possible to sustain.[22]

How can we talk about community and virtue in a society that prizes self-absorbed individualism? How can we teach our children the worth of the cardinal virtues in a society that tells them human flourishing is the person with the most money and material goods, success is having the sort of job that will ensure one the most money, and human excellence is any action that makes one a "winner," even if winning involves stepping on or destroying others who get in the way?

Sharon Parks suggests that our young people have too few "networks of belonging," i.e., too few places in which to ask the questions and dream the dreams necessary to equip them with the moral imagination required to be good citizens in a global society.[23] Before one can ask such questions and dream such dreams, one has to have a context in which to care about other people. Only in relationship to others, only in community, do we find the context to develop morality.

Conversely, morality is required for community to remain intact. Alan Gerwith tells us that

A morality may be defined as a set of rules or directives for actions and institutions, especially as these are held to support or uphold what are taken to be the most important values or interests of persons other than or in addition to the agent. The rules are held to be categorically obligatory in that compliance with them is held to be mandatory regardless of one's personal inclinations or institutional affiliations.[24]

Without the "categorically obligatory" rules, the community would be destroyed. Thus community requires morality.

Human Purpose and the Cardinal Virtues

If, as Gerwith suggests, community requires that its members adhere to some basic moral tenets that hold for everyone, and if that morality requires community as a context for meaningful, understandable development and linguistic codification, why should we bother with either morality or community? Why go to so much trouble? Why not descend into the chaos and anarchy that would result if every person was a self-absorbed individualist completely oblivious to the needs and rights of others?

I believe that without an understanding of human purpose, we cannot adequately determine a reason for engaging in either community or morality. Though we have lost the context for our moral language, we still have the rhetoric and a sense of the importance of moral issues. However, we no longer have a sense of our purpose as a community of people.

Therefore, we must determine what the purpose of being human is. Aristotle thought human purpose was twofold: 1) to know the truth and 2) to construct and live in a society. Within this context, moral virtues would be those skills, inclinations, habits, dispositions, and abilities that enable persons to discover truth and to live in social harmony.[25] Four virtues, in particular, came to the fore in ancient Greek society: prudence, justice, fortitude, and temperance. Known as the four cardinal virtues or the "doctrine of virtue," they were included in Plato's *Symposium* as part of the character Agathon's speech in praise of Love.[26]

Two of these cardinal virtues, prudence and justice, give humans the capacity to pursue the good directly. As classically understood, prudence is the capacity to see the world truthfully and thus to choose well the path that will take one toward one's goal. Justice is the capacity to take due account of the claims of others, whether friends or enemies, whether they help or harm one's interests.[27]

The other two cardinal virtues, courage and temperance, give humans the capacity to pursue the good indirectly; they clear the way for the good to be pursued. Again, the classical understanding of courage is that it is the willingness to forfeit or place at risk genuine goods for the sake of a greater good. Temperance, classically understood, is that ordering of one's appetites for real goods so that they achieve the goods at which they are aimed.[28]

It is important to note that virtues cannot be reduced to rules. Rules and laws are what we fall back on when the virtues fail, when we have lost other ways of shaping and judging behavior.[29] But because virtues cannot be reduced to rules and because we have lost the classical context through which to understand the cardinal virtues, we are awash in a sea of moral ambiguity that tries to make sense of the language of virtue within the contemporary cultural context. This results in interpretations exactly opposite, in some cases, of the classical understanding of prudence, justice, courage, and temperance.

Take, for example, prudence, which initially was considered to be a prerequisite for goodness. In the contemporary mind, prudence more often means evasion or avoidance of a situation or danger. Conventional wisdom informs us that such behavior is merely common sense. For example, the wise person is *prudent* to evade personal commitment or avoid placing oneself at risk. By contrast, "classical Christian ethics . . . maintains that man [sic] can be prudent and good only simultaneously; that prudence is part and parcel of the definition of goodness."[30]

The ambiguity resulting from the loss of the classical context for the virtues led to the development of *emotivism*, "the doctrine that all evaluative judgments and more specifically all moral judgments are *nothing but* expressions of preference, expressions of attitude or feeling, insofar as they are moral or evaluative in character."[31]

Emotivism would view self-absorbed individualism as just one more expression of preference regarding the way to determine good or right action. Currently, much of American society lauds individualism that sees individual fulfillment, even at the expense of others, as the primary purpose of living.

But, if the primary purpose of being human is to be in relationship with other humans and with God, an ethic of self-absorbed individualism is neither prudent nor moral. Thus, we are back to the question of what the primary purpose of being human is, for we cannot understand virtue except in the context of what it means to be human and what constitutes human flourishing.

In the Judeo-Christian tradition, interpretation of the text of Genesis 1:27, which tells us God created humankind in God's own image, generated the concept of *imitatio dei*. That is, if we are created in the image of God (*imago dei*) then surely we are called to imitate God. "Human images have a responsibility to behave in God-like ways, to walk in God's paths and imitate God's actions . . . Paul states this bluntly, exhorting the people to be imitators of God (Eph. 5:1) and to 'be imitators of me as I am of Christ' (1 Cor. 11:1)."[32] Daniel Migliore tells us that "every view of what it means to be truly human implies a certain understanding of what God is, and every understanding of what is divine issues in a particular view of what it means to be human."[33]

Consequently, if we understand God to be love, as Christian scripture plainly states (1 John 4:8b), then humans are created to "be love" or "to love" as well. This cannot occur in isolation; love requires relationship. To act according to the purpose for which we were created, we must be in relationship with God and with one another. Humans do not truly reflect the image of the Trinitarian God except when we are united with one another. The Divine dance requires relationship. As Jurgen Moltmann says, "Likeness to God cannot be lived in isolation. It can be lived only in human community."[34]

To help us achieve community, God gave us two primary commandments, "You shall love the Lord your God with all your heart, with all your mind, with all your soul, and you shall love your neighbor as yourself" (Matthew 22:37–39). Whether or not the self-absorbed individualist loves him/herself, such a person is definitely concerned primarily with the well-being of self over that of others, directly violating the command to love one's neighbor as one's self. I believe this sort of individualism is immoral both because "morality requires interpersonal consideration whereby each person must be concerned for the important interests of other persons besides himself or herself,"[35] and because moral life is a process of becoming through which we are fitted for the bliss of friendship with God. Individualism leads to alienation, actually diminishes one's stature, and deprives the community of one's gifts. It also prevents one from developing the virtues, the skills, actions, habits, etc., that lead us toward communion with one another and with God.

The Rise of Individualism

Individualism is a fairly recent concept in human understanding of identity. In heroic societies, the self was defined by a person's role in society; individualism was a nonconcept.[36] However, by the seventeenth century, human egoism had been recognized as a problem, one to which morality could offer a solution.[37] Then, in the eighteenth century, the Enlightenment brought a new emphasis on rationalism and objectivism. Human behavior was now thought to be predictable which meant it could be manipulated and controlled.[38] The Enlightment gave birth to the individual.[39]

In the nineteenth century Alexis de Tocqueville published *Democracy in America* in which he described the undergirding mores or social practices that gave this country a unique new culture. The characteristic that he found most normative was our individualism. Tocqueville thought this was an admirable trait, but "he very clearly warned that unless our individualism was continually and strongly balanced by other habits, it would inevitably lead to fragmentation of American society and social isolation of its citizens."[40]

Parker Palmer has identified such fragmentation and isolation in the academy. He writes, "I call the pain that permeates education the 'pain of disconnection.' Everywhere I go, I meet faculty who feel disconnected from their colleagues, from their students, and from their own hearts."[41]

Peck, Bellah, Gorman, and MacIntyre are among a number of authors who view the fragmentation of human life that has indeed come about as a genuine moral problem. Bellah describes modernity as a "culture of separation" that will collapse from its own incoherence if it ever becomes completely dominant.[42] MacIntyre adds that

> A virtue is now generally understood as a disposition or sentiment which will produce in us obedience to certain rules; agreement on what the relevant rules are to be is always a prerequisite for agreement upon the nature and content of a particular virtue. But this prior agreement in rules is . . . something which our individualist culture is unable to secure.[43]

Each role we play, each activity in which we engage now comes with its own codes of conduct, its own behavioral norms. These behavioral norms are usually focused on self-fulfillment and personal success which leads to an ever-increasing fragmentation of our lives. "The drive for self-fulfillment reveals our preoccupation with personal autonomy and separateness. In our culture individualism is king and generates pride. Our heroes are those who made it on their own or survived to make it to the top of the heap by standing on others."[44] Peck takes the dramatic step of claiming that "any form of behavior that stems from lack of integration, that represents compartmentalization, is blasphemy," and "the degree of compartmentalization in American life is such that blasphemous behavior is the norm rather than the exception."[45]

Self-Absorbed Individualism and the Cardinal Virtues

Gilbert Meilander has written that today's cardinal virtues are "sincerity and authenticity—in short, being true to oneself."[46] These may be virtues that are possible for a modern-day individualist to develop because they focus on the self. But upon closer examination, I think we will discover that they are contrary to the actual behaviors of a self-absorbed individualist. Sincerity comes from the Latin roots *cine* (without) and *cero* (wax). In ancient times disreputable art dealers would hide the flaws and imperfections in sculptures with wax. So to be without wax, *cine cero*, implied honesty and truth.[47] Sincerity continues to have the implications of honesty and truth, which are the opposite of the lying and deception a self-absorbed individualist would not be hesitant to engage in if it meant keeping self in the winner's box.

Likewise, authenticity implies a genuineness or trustworthiness—a sincerity that is not attributable to the self-centered individualist as he/she has been described in the literature examined for this book. It is, however, intriguing to note that a Latin derivative of the root *authentic-cus* is *authentes* which means "one who does things himself."[48]

The traditional cardinal virtues do not fare any better with the modern-day individualism. For example, if prudence is the capacity to see the world truthfully and thus to choose well the path that will take one toward one's goal, then the self-aggrandizing individualist cannot be prudent because he/she does not see the world truthfully; his/her worldview is distorted by the extreme focus on self above all else, leading the individualist to choose the paths that move him/her toward the goal of self-fulfillment.

By definition, the self-absorbed individualist is focused on the flourishing of self at the expense of others if necessary; that is, the claims of others are not important to this person except as they may pose a threat to or shield for his/her success. Therefore, justice, the capacity to take due account of the claims of others, whether friends or enemies, whether they help or harm one's interests, is antithetical to self-absorbed individualism, for the individualist will only give credence to the friends and enemies whose claims further his/her own flourishing. "The core of justice in all times and places is care for the neighbor."[49] Significantly, the most frequently occurring word in the Christian Gospel is *neighbor*.[50] But the only person the self-absorbed individualist cares about is self; a neighbor comes into consideration only with regard to the ways in which the neighbor can provide benefit.

What about the virtue of courage? The mental image wrought by the term *individualist* certainly could conjure a person of courage. But the courage it takes to stand against all others for the prospering of self is hardly the sort of courage that is among the moral virtues. As a virtue, courage is the willingness to forfeit or place at risk genuine goods for the sake of a greater good, such as placing the self at risk for the sake of community. For the self-absorbed individualist, the reason to be in community is not to contribute to the common good but to reap whatever personal rewards such association might offer.

Finally, let us consider the virtue of temperance, that ordering of one's appetites for real goods so that they achieve the goods at which they are aimed. With only this definition of temperance on which to base a judgment, the individualist could, I suppose, be said to be temperate. In fact, the individualist excels at ordering his/her appetites for what he/she perceives as real goods so that these goods are attained. But the clue here lies in perception and, as noted above, the individualist's view of reality is totally distorted by self-interest.

The cardinal virtues were born in a context of community. It is only in modern society that the heresy of individualistic interpretations of prudence, justice, courage, and temperance could occur. Thus self-absorbed individualism cannot be said to display any of the cardinal virtues as they have been traditionally understood. The idolatrous focus on self distorts truth, disrupts social harmony, and does nothing to foster relationships with others or with God. The self-absorbed individualist has no interest in fulfilling the purpose of being human as this purpose was identified at the beginning of this chapter. The only human purpose he/she finds valid is personal fulfillment. Therefore, when our culture validates such individualism as an admirable and desirable way of being in the world, it necessarily invalidates the usefulness and merit of the cardinal virtues and is totally blind to our primary human purpose of being in community with others and in communion with God. The ethic of self-absorbed individualism transmitted by our culture makes moral formation for anyone countercultural.

Self-Absorbed Individualism:
Culturally Instilled, Transmitted, and Valued

Conventional wisdom consists of the understandings of reality that a culture takes for granted. Marcus Borg suggests it is "the dominant consciousness of any culture . . . the world that everybody is socialized into through the process of growing up . . . the consciousness shaped and structured by culture or tradition."[51] This is the sort of wisdom that is often encapsulated on bumper stickers and in advertising slogans. Consider the following list:

> First place is the only one that counts.
> Pull yourself up by your own bootstraps.
> Anyone can succeed if he/she really tries.
> If people are poor it's their own fault.
> Stand on your own two feet.
> Just do it.
> Be all that you can be.
> I'll take the cake; you can have the crumbs—but there won't be any crumbs!
> The one who dies with the most toys wins.
> Winner take all!
> Don't just keep up with the Joneses—get ahead of them!
> Love is for wimps!
> Be your own boss.
> Nice guys finish last.

This list is derived from my own encounters with bumper stickers, newspapers, magazines, television, and radio, i.e., public media. All of them point to the value of the individual. None of them values community. Gorman offers additional examples of conventional wisdom:

> From our youth we have been taught such axioms as "Don't depend on anyone else," "Decide on your own," "If you don't look out for yourself, nobody will," "Stand on your own two feet." We have embraced freedom of choice as the highest virtue. We prize the license to move in and out of relationships based on our own decisions. . . . If the relationship does not fulfill us—whether friendship, group, church, marriage or other—we can opt out.[52]

A sort of rugged individualism actually may have been necessary for survival in the early days of the American frontier that spawned cultural heroes like Daniel Boone, Davy Crockett, and Andrew Jackson. In those days, people were truly isolated by distance. Those who lived a day's journey or more from their closest neighbors often needed to be self-sufficient.

Stories from the frontier grew into cultural myths that made heroes out of those who were rugged enough to survive. As the west developed, the American cowboy joined the ranks of rugged individualists who could stand alone without the need to depend on others. As cities grew and crime rates increased, detectives like Dick Tracy, Mike Hammer, and Dirty Harry were integrated into the cultural myths as characters who depended on their own judgment and refused to submit to the wishes of others because they preferred doing things their own way.[53]

Recognizing the fortune to be made in bringing comic book superheroes to life, movie makers produced series about Batman, Superman, Spiderman, and the Incredible Hulk, all rugged individualists who are self-sufficient, courageous, and who fight alone for "truth, justice, and the American Way." The more human, though equally fantastic, forms of movie superheroes appeared in films such as *Rambo*, *The Terminator*, the Jackie Chan series and various versions of "Agent 007." Admittedly these cultural icons often act selflessly, taking risks to rescue those in distress without thought of personal safety. However, they also encourage a degree of vigilantism that is dangerous to the structure of society that is dependent on behavioral rules and laws to maintain social order. Movies starring such heroes communicate values as surely as any other forms of storytelling, and MacIntyre reminds us that storytelling, in classical moral thinking, was a primary means of moral education.[54]

I believe stories function to raise our awareness and affect our perception of reality in three primary ways. Stories can act as lenses that help us see more clearly or take a closer look at something. They can also operate like windows, helping us see beyond the boundaries of our immediate perceptions. Additionally, they can function as mirrors, reflecting back to us who we are or who we ought to become. In the case of our cultural superhero myths, the function is mostly mirror, reflecting back to us that we need to be strong, courageous individuals, not afraid to take the law into our own hands when necessary and not averse to encouraging violence as a means to a sought after end.

In the last few years a number of television shows that promote this extreme form of individualism have become popular. These include *Survivor* and *Fear Factor*. *Survivor* is particularly insidious because it puts people together in pseudo-community and then requires the group to periodically vote a member out. The "winner" is the last person to survive not only various environmental challenges but the group's dynamics. The prize is twofold. The survivor becomes a publicly acknowledged rugged individualist and he/she receives an enormous financial payoff.

Such programs teach us a number of life lessons. We learn that to be a "winner" or to survive, we must not trust one another, even those whom we may have depended on in the past. We must not value community. We are ultimately alone in this tough world and we must be the strongest, most physically fit, meanest, and best to survive. Compassion will cause us to lose. On campus these ideas are lived out in temporary "friendships" that are valued only as long as they meet one's personal needs. Relationships become "'things' to be selected and rejected at our convenience."[55]

I firmly believe that rugged individualism, a holdover from a frontier culture of long distances and isolation, is counterproductive in twenty-first-century society. In this age of efficient transportation, high-speed communication, transoceanic teleconferencing, and ever-growing population densities, few of us are truly isolated. The ethic of rugged individualism that once may have contributed to human survival now only risks contributing to global annihilation. One simply cannot acquire a morality that favors community if one's primary worldview requires one to be a survivor, putting the good of self above the good of others. Thus, the myth of the self-sufficient individualistic hero must be exposed as contrary to human thriving if one is to offer moral education to persons raised in a culture that holds self-absorbed individualism as a primary paradigm for successful living—a paradigm that threatens the entire ecology of life on earth.

Currently in our culture success appears to involve two elements: 1) progress toward economic self-sufficiency and 2) increased personal choice. Success implies the accomplishment of individual goals and ambitions—with little time to develop community and personal relationships. We are constantly trying to measure up to the standards dictated by the culture. Our preoccupation with productivity and "getting ahead" has made us extremely competitive. Gorman warns that "competition is a handmaid to individualism, and competition in America is as normative as baseball and apple pie."[56]

Our out-of-control competition often leads us to define ourselves, and one another, by what we do rather than who we are—because we do not take time to discover who we are, nor whose we are. Too many students come to college not for an education but to get a good job. In the mid-twentieth century Robert Bellah found that "for middle-class Americans, a calculating attitude toward educational and occupational choice has been essential and has often spilled over into determining our criteria for the choice of spouse, friends, and voluntary associations."[57] If anything, this "calculating attitude" has grown worse in a culture that values winners over losers and creates a dichotomy of competition that precludes the elimination of losers as a category into which some of us must necessarily fall.

Students' focus on careers is mirrored in the academy itself as economic concerns rise with falling investment incomes and institutions feel a need to market themselves to prospective students who are now seen as consumers.[58] Like students who are concerned with getting "good" jobs (i.e., jobs that pay well), the academy has become increasingly focused on profit making; too often educating students and serving their general welfare seem to have become secondary. Walter Wink suggests that when an institution pursues a purpose other than that for which it was created it has become idolatrous and its actions demonic.[59] I think the same can be said of humans when we pursue a purpose other than that for which we were created. In order to know how to act we must rediscover why we are here.

Opposing Voices

I believe the need for community—individually, among groups, among nations, among the world's religions—has never been greater than it is now in what, through the wonders of technology, is becoming a global society. But before exploring possibilities that might lead us along paths toward the development of community in ever-widening circles, I must address objections that surely will be raised by those who do not agree with the foundations of my thesis.

Some may raise the issue that while self-absorbed individualism may well be a cultural icon it is not a pervasive problem. I would disagree on several levels. If self-absorbed individualism is a cultural icon, and I believe that I have shown that to be the case, then it is by definition pervasive in our culture. Additionally, since it is contrary to the formation and functioning of community which is required for the formation of morality, and since morality is required for the maintenance of community which is the very basis of being in relationship with each other and with God, self-centered individualism is very much a problem, one that thwarts the individual's ability and desire to fulfill his/her human purpose.

A second objection might be that while self-absorbed individualism may be a cultural icon it is certainly not a universally held value. I agree. Some of us are countercultural in the values we hold—thank goodness! But many who would raise this objection on the basis that they are not self-absorbed individualists because they are in relationship with others through their church, civic club, or other organization, may well be subject to the effect this core cultural value can have on entire groups of people. For example, I may be a member of a religious or political group that is convinced that it holds the only truth. My group then functions as a self-absorbed individualist, focused on its personal flourishing and survival at the expense of all others. Its members are in community with one another but the group is not in community with the larger society.

Because so much of my focus is on the benefits of community and its necessity for human moral development, let me acknowledge here that community can also be very, very dangerous. When a community becomes coercive rather than voluntary, when it functions as a mind-numbing cult, when it engages in behaviors that are not life-giving to its members (e.g., the Jim Jones and Heaven's Gate cults) or to the society at large, or when community favors some of its members and marginalizes others (e.g., racism, ageism, heterosexism), community is a negative thing. It has become self-absorbed.

Even entire nations of people can function as self-absorbed individualists who consider their version of the "truth" the only valid one. My own country has embraced self-absorbed individualism to the point that it sees itself as the holder of the only real political truth and, like the world-saving heroes from ancient fable to modern movie, acts as if its well-being is not interrelated with the well-being of other nations. While the decision to invade Iraq was and has continued to be couched in moral terms of justice, increased prospects for peace, human dignity, and freedom, I cannot escape the sense that economics and the core value of rugged individualism are the actual underlying motivations shaping a foreign policy that says, "We'd better get ours and the rest of the world can have whatever is left." Humanity cannot survive if nations cannot learn to live together despite our differences, embracing our differences, in community.[60]

Another version of the objection that "self-absorbed individualism is not a universally held value" would be "self-absorbed individualism is not the only core value of our culture. What about traditional family values?" On the face of it, I have no quarrel with "traditional family values." I think families are important and can provide excellent moral instruction. But I must ask what is a traditional family and what were/are its values? Do these values contribute to the common good of all or only to the common good of persons who hold the values? Remembering Gerwith's "Principle of Generic Consistency," all of us have the right to freedom and well-being.[61] Yet from what I know of the traditional family values movement, gays, lesbians, bisexuals, and transgendered persons are not to be afforded certain rights (such as same sex unions) because their values supposedly are at odds with those of the traditional family.[62]

Another obvious objection would come from those who claim to be atheists. If one does not believe in the existence of God, then one of my foundational premises, that the purpose of being human is to be in relationship with others and with God, is inherently meaningless. I would respond to that by suggesting that humans cannot live meaningfully without relationships. Bellah tells us that "it is only in relation to society that the individual can fulfill himself and, if the break with society is too radical, life has no meaning at all."[63] More recently, Carlos Ball noted that "it is our interacting with others, as well as our dependencies on others, that allow us to lead lives that are fully human."[64] Human companionship is a basic human need. This is true even if one is an atheist. Whether or not one believes in God, one still requires relationships in order to be human; one still requires community in order to develop morality.

A fourth objection may come in the form of the claim that "I have a right to my individualism." Perhaps; certainly we all have the God-given freedom to choose whether or not to be in relationship with others. But I believe that freedom comes with a certain amount of responsibility and "'I have my rights' is at the opposite end of the spectrum from 'I have responsibility.'"[65] "I have my rights" is a statement that one might expect from those who prize individualism. "I have responsibility" comes from persons who have accepted the moral obligations necessary for living together in community.

"It has pleased God to transmit life through relationships."[66] Therefore, individualism is contrary to God's system. Most, if not all the world's religions teach that the self-centered life is detrimental to the flourishing of the human spirit because the self whose life and world are egocentric fails "to view the human situation from the perspective of the unifying center of the ultimate and is not responsive to the normative conditions and requirements of the total context of human existence."[67]

Creating a Paradigm Shift

Is it possible to change our core cultural value of self-absorbed individualism? Is there some way to create a new paradigm for human thriving (or to reconnect with one from the past that values living together in mutual relationship)? If it is possible to effect such change, one shift we as a culture will have to make is from being in competition with one another to cooperating with each other. We will need to stop valuing personal achievement and acquisition over helping one another thrive.

In one of the richest (at least economically) nations in the world, we are raising children who equate money with achievement. "We live as if our happiness depended on having."[68] Tex Sample calls achievement our civil religion in which "winning is god, and adherents of the religion worship at a pyramidal altar where striving is endless because every success becomes a failure for not having done better."[69] In such an environment the concept of vocation, that which one feels called to do with one's life, gets lost in a culturally determined sense of destiny that gives advice on how to be a winner.[70] Too often careerism causes people to choose jobs that are contrary to their nature.

I believe the academy is in a significant position to educate students in the concept of vocation, countercultural though it may be, such that seeking meaningful employment takes precedence over seeking lucrative employment. I also believe our colleges and universities have the opportunity and responsibility for the development of persons who value community over self-absorbed individualism. While I agree with Meilander who says that trying to instruct a student's conscience is a "high calling,"[71] I believe we who are privileged to teach in the academy ignore this vital aspect of human development at their peril—and our own.

> The liberally educated person, many now argue, needs not only substantial knowledge but also the skills and awareness to negotiate what Maxine Greene has called "a world lived in common with others." Thus colleges and universities must educate not in terms of mind alone but also in terms of life lived in relationships with others whose experiences and assumptions may be very different.[72]

I believe a primary purpose of the academy is to educate its students in order to equip them for meaningful lives as citizens in a global society. Therefore, I also believe the academy must accept responsibility for the moral education of young adults to help them resist the insidious individualism that is the core value of current culture. "Successful moral education requires a community which does not hesitate to inculcate virtue in the young, which does not settle for the discordant opinions of alternate visions of the good. . . ."[73] Morality is not a matter of private choice and personal taste as our culture would have us believe.

Creating the openings that allow space for these major mental shifts will require, at least in part, providing what Sharon Parks has named "networks of belonging."[74] These networks may be cocurricular or they may be created in interdisciplinary classrooms, but they need to offer alternative epistemologies that both encourage the exploration of values and recognize that knowing has a spiritual dimension.[75]

One means of teaching virtue is storytelling.[76] I have already discussed the major functions of story and the community-defeating messages transmitted by the various media portrayals of the rugged individualist. Parker Palmer believes that "students would learn more true lessons about the nature of life on all levels if we were to shape our schools around images of reality that are less individualistic and competitive and more cooperative and communal . . . scholars now understand that knowing is a profoundly communal act."[77]

If storytelling is such a powerful tool in moral formation, and if we agree that students need "networks of belonging," then perhaps the academy should pursue the creation of safe space for students to engage in sharing their stories and reflecting upon them. We might have to help them learn to listen to their lives as stories, for MacIntyre maintains that "to think of a life as a narrative unity is to think in a way alien to the dominant individualist and bureaucratic modes of modern culture."[78] But the effort required is surely worthwhile.

In these groups students would also have a space in which it is safe to learn to ask the right questions. Our culture has taught them to ask, "What's in it for me?" rather than "How might this affect my neighbor and me together?" Instead of focusing on how to find a high-paying job, students need to learn to ask "What is a good life?" and "How do we know?" They need spaces in which to discover their hearts and connect them to their minds so they can ask, "What in life is worth giving my heart to?"

Spiritual life retreats, particularly if they are held in a location away from the campus, are ideally suited to offering safe space for the formation of story groups. Through connecting their own stories to the stories that have nurtured people of faith through the ages, students begin to see how they are part of the larger narrative. Through discovering stories common to several faiths, students can begin to focus on similarities rather than only on differences between their faith and that of another.

One of the most formative experiences of my own life was writing an essay in response to the question, "What is your lost sheep?" In other words, for what was I willing to risk everything else in order to go after it? While campus ministries do not usually ask students to write essays, there is no reason students could not be asked to reflect on important questions such as this in personal journals or periods of silence kept in retreat settings. Then, during times of gathered community the students can reflect together on the insights gained from their experience.

Of course sharing personal stories and reflections involves risk. It makes us vulnerable to one another. But that is one reason taking the risk is so important. Unless we can take a chance on exposing our vulnerabilities, we cannot experience any sort of mutual relationship. Gorman notes that "every act of authentic self-disclosure makes one person's story a gift to the growth of another. When we genuinely understand another person's story, we grow as individuals and our spiritual nature is magnified."[79]

Sharing our stories in small groups made safe through agreed-upon covenants of confidentiality can free us to finally experience real community, "a state of being together in which people, instead of hiding behind their defenses, learn to lower them, in which instead of attempting to obliterate their differences, people learn not only to accept them but rejoice in them."[80]

Whatever is to be done to create a cultural paradigm shift will, I believe, come from some sort of communal experience, some network of belonging in which we are finally free to take off our suffocating individual masks and breathe. Of course, it is possible that such small communities could become isolated pockets— group-sized "individuals" who value themselves alone. As John Winthrop of the Massachusetts Bay Colony stated in a sermon preached just before the colonists set foot on land, "We must delight in each other, make other's conditions our own, rejoice together, mourn together, labor and suffer together, always having before our eyes our community as members of the same body."[81] But we must understand that the human community of which we are all members is the entirety of humankind.

We humans find it difficult to think beyond our own self interests,[82] partly because we do not have a deep sense of connection with one another and our environment; too often we do not grasp that what happens to one of us in some sense happens to all of us. The Apostle Paul recognized this as the problem the members of the church at Corinth were having in the first century. Some self-absorbed individuals were acting as if some members of the congregation were less important than others and might even be excluded. Paul used the metaphor of the church as the body of Christ to illustrate the fallacious nature of such thinking.

> The eye cannot say to the hand, "I have no need of you," nor again the head to the feet, "I have no need of you." On the contrary, the members of the body that seem to be weaker are indispensable, and those members of the body that we think less honorable we clothe with greater honor, and our less respectable members are treated with greater respect; whereas our more respectable members do not need this. But God has so arranged the body, giving the greater honor to the inferior member, that there may be no dissension within the body, but the members may have the same care for one another. If one member suffers, all suffer together with it; if one member is honored, all rejoice together with it. Now you are the body of Christ and individually members of it (1 Corinthians 12:21–27).

As creatures of a compassionate creator, we are called to become compassionate. We are called to care for our neighbors, other creatures, and our environment, not just for ourselves or our particular group. As we work together to create a new core cultural value, "What matters at this stage is the construction of local forms of community within which civility and the intellectual and moral life can be sustained through the new dark ages which are already upon us."[83]

It has been my experience that taking students on weekend spiritual life retreats helps to shape communities that would otherwise not have been formed. In the campus dining hall, students tend to sit in homogeneous groups: Christians with other Christians, Muslims with other Muslims, African Americans with other African Americans, international students with other international students, athletes with other athletes, fraternity and sorority members with other Greeks. At spiritual life retreats in which Christians, Muslims, Buddhists, and Jews are all together in a relatively small group (twenty to twenty-five students) that cooks together, eats together, studies together, sleeps together, plays together, and creates together, students begin to appreciate the richness their diversity offers the small community and they begin to build relationships that last even after they graduate. They also begin to broaden their understanding of the Divine as true mystery that cannot possibly be entirely captured by the metaphors of any single religion.

TWO

Creating Community in an Interfaith Environment

Adaptive Challenges

Creating, shaping, and getting college students to participate in interfaith retreats is an *adaptive challenge* for campus ministry in the twenty-first century. Ronald Heifetz defines an *adaptive challenge* as "a particular kind of problem where the gap [between values and circumstances] cannot be closed by the application of current technical know-how or routine behavior."[1] Heifetz is specifically thinking of adaptations necessary for effective leadership. While "technical know-how" is certainly important in the design and leadership of interfaith retreats, the adaptive challenge in this case lies with the need to change routine behavior.

Human beings can be incredibly xenophobic and tend to gravitate toward that which is familiar. In the largely Christian environment of a college with a Presbyterian heritage such as the one I serve as Chaplain, non-Christian theologies are often seen as threatening to the status quo and their articulation creates ambiguity at a developmental juncture when young people find ambiguity to be anathema. To avoid the ambiguity of exposure to religious ideas that differ from their own, many students try routinely to avoid contact with persons of other faiths. In so doing, they deny themselves the opportunity to deepen their own faith by learning about that of others. Students (and the rest of us) need to understand that "diversity does not necessarily signify contradiction; it can simply betoken otherness, another way of being human."[2]

Heifetz argues that in order to respond to an adaptive challenge, invention and change must occur in circumstances, in values held, or in both.[3] Interfaith retreats offer a change in circumstances, taking students away from the immediate campus environment and putting persons of differing faiths together in more closely shared space with opportunities to engage in common, community building experience such as table-sharing, dialogue, playing, and undertaking creative arts together. At such retreats I have seen students focus more on what they have in common than on how they differ from one another, including discovery of values and ethics that are common across faith traditions. Heifetz asks, "Are there shared values that might help us engage competing views?"[4] I believe there are; we need only have the courage to challenge what too often our religions would have us believe—that the particular tradition in which we were raised or to which we now cling is the only one that is right and true, and other people must proclaim the same understanding or be forever damned.

Such narrow thinking seems almost genetically encoded as some sort of survival mechanism in human beings. We rarely question what Marcus Borg calls *conventional wisdom* or *enculturated consciousness*.[5] As noted in my discussion of self-absorbed individualism in chapter 2, conventional wisdom transmits the central values and behavioral rules of a culture; it supplies the framework necessary for getting along. It is the programmer of our internal cop and judge and is seldom challenged.[6]

Marcus Borg's *conventional wisdom* would be described by Bolman and Deal as belonging to the *symbolic frame*, that which "focuses on how humans make sense of the messy, ambiguous world in which they live."[7] Ways of making meaning that lie within the symbolic frame are tremendously difficult to change because symbols communicate in ways that lie outside the boundaries of rationality and certainty while opening us to a deeper reality in which the symbols themselves participate.[8]

A third description of this phenomenon can be found in the work of Mihaly Csikszentmihalyi who categorizes symbolic ways of knowing into *domains*. He suggests that:

> Knowledge mediated by symbols is extrasomatic; it is not transmitted through chemical codes inscribed in our chromosomes but must be intentionally passed on and learned. It is this extrasomatic knowledge conveyed by symbols that makes up what we call a culture. And the knowledge conveyed by symbols is bundled up in discreet domains—geometry, music, religion, legal systems, and so on. Each domain is made up of its own symbolic elements, its own rules, and generally has its own system of notation. In many ways, each domain describes an isolated little world in which a person can think and act with clarity and concentration.[9]

Yet a fourth way of approaching this concept of frameworks that help us organize our understandings is offered by Walter Wink in his discussion of *worldviews*:

> A worldview dictates the way whole societies see the world. . . . As I am using the term, worldviews are not philosophies, theologies, or even myths or tales about the origin of things. They are the barebones structures with which we think. They are the foundation of the house of our minds on which we erect symbols, myths, and systems of thought . . . normally a worldview functions on an unconscious level. People are unaware of its existence. It is just the way things are.[10]

The worldview of a culture is comprised of understandings that are simply taken for granted—basic concepts of reality that help us know how to live.[11]

Every religion has its own conventional wisdom, symbolic frame, worldview, or domain with rules and symbols. Sometimes these aspects of religion dominate an entire culture such that the world thinks of a particular country as primarily Islamic, or Christian, or Hindu. When this is the case, as arguably it is at a Presbyterian college in a culture which, at least historically, has been thought of as Christian, then challenging conventional wisdom becomes a challenge to religion as well. My students are often shocked by the idea that religious tradition not only should be questioned but that it can actually be wrong. When they are confronted with the possibility that things have not always been the way they are now, especially with regard to religious dogma, beliefs, and values, their frames of reference are shifted, cracked—or even shattered. Parks notes that:

> They [young adults] are functioning within various systems upon which they have very little if any critical purchase. That is, they may have the capacity for critical thought, but they use it only within certain limited frames—unable to question the frame itself.[12]

Christian students are simultaneously fascinated and horrified to discover similarities between Christian ideas and those of much older religions, such as Zoroastrianism, from which some Christian beliefs appear to have been borrowed.[13] They are shocked to learn that church leaders once argued over whether or not Jesus was divine and that the concept of the Trinity was not a part of Christianity from the beginning.[14]

This brings us full circle, back to Heifetz' discussion of adaptive challenge at the heart of which, he suggests, is often "the testing and changing of perceptions."[15] It is not surprising that Heifetz labels adaptive work a *challenge*; he recognizes that leading others into areas that require adaptive change often provokes fear, "particularly if the stakes are high."[16] Probably few, if any, stakes are higher than one's religious beliefs and values.

The Need for Adaptive Change

"People who lead frequently bear scars from their efforts to bring about adaptive change."[17] Knowing this, why would anyone be so bold as to challenge their campus community with an adaptive change? My own courage comes in part from already having been bloodied; I bear the scars from the reactions of some of the citizens of a small Midwestern town, including some of its religious leaders, following a campus 9/11 memorial service in September 2002. In this service my students and I dared to offer prayers and readings from all faiths, including Wicca, which was the one that sparked the subsequent explosion.

We had done our homework and knew which faiths were represented among the dead. We thought there might be a negative reaction from some of the more conservative Christians on campus; never in our wildest dreams did we expect the local citizens to even notice, much less become outraged. But we had challenged "the barebones structures" of their thinking. Parks reminds us that:

> Individually and collectively, we long for a trustworthy, dependable equilibrium in a dynamic, roiling world. This longing is one way of understanding some of the tremendous attraction of fundamentalist religion at this time in history.[18]

The reaction to our 9/11 memorial service serves to emphasize the importance of interfaith dialogue and experience for our students, lest they emerge from their college years equally as limited in their ability to accept the ideas of others.

Part of the threat surely lies in the conventional wisdom that acceptance means agreement. It does not. I can accept—and learn from—the concepts and ideas of other religions without agreeing with them and adopting them as my own. One of the primary gifts of participation in an interfaith spiritual retreat is the opportunity for students to talk with people of different faiths. Invariably students' evaluations of their retreat experiences include statements like, "In talking with people of other faiths about their beliefs, I found new strength in my own" (see Appendices I and J). Dettling attests to similar experience:

> When I open myself up to interreligious conversation, I recognise [sic] a convergence with Jesus' own way of life. He too opened himself to the world around him, and gave himself up for all people. It is only through His kind of openness that a person can begin to understand, indeed can want to understand. It involves two things: the attempt to understand what is different, and a fidelity to one's own faith.[19]

Heifetz claims that "adaptive work consists of the learning required to address conflicts in the values people hold, or to diminish the gap between the values people stand for and the reality they face."[20] Many people, including me, hold Christian values. But the reality we face is that most of the world is not Christian. Being responsible for campus ministry in the multi-faith environment found today on most campuses presents an adaptive challenge. I believe Christian campus ministries that fail to offer students opportunities to learn about and dialogue with persons from other religious traditions are not meeting the needs of students who will graduate to become citizens of a global society.

Another, and perhaps less demanding, adaptive challenge results from what I believe is a need in higher education to offer alternatives to Enlightenment thinking, epistemologies that both encourage the exploration of values and recognize that knowing has a spiritual dimension.[21] Jon Dalton suggests that:

> Higher education that ignores the spiritual dimension of learning and development not only inhibits students' quest for the good life but it makes it less likely that graduates will be engaged citizens willing to do the long and arduous work of creating a good society.[22]

It is time the academy stopped suffering from the objectivism wrought by the Enlightenment, for "objectivism, far from telling the truth about how we know, is a myth meant to feed our fading fantasy of science, technology, power, and control."[23] To leave the subjective, the spiritual, the intuitive, the imaginative out of the academy is to educate only a part of the knowing self. Training students to value only the objective is to risk denying them experience of their full humanity.[24] As Marcus Borg notes:

> Visions happen, enlightenment experiences happen, paranormal experiences happen. These experiences suggest that reality is far more mysterious than any and all of our domestications—whether scientific or religious—make it out to be. They suggest that reality is more, much more, than modernity has imagined.[25]

The primary way we humans have of making sense out of the "much more than modernity has imagined" is through the use of symbols.

The Power and Function of Symbols

Living organisms, including humans, respond to stimuli from the world with more or less built-in mechanisms. But humans uniquely also have the capacity "to open up new perspectives on reality based on information mediated by symbols."[26] Worldviews, religions, domains, and cultures all involve what Csikszentmihalyi called "extrasomatic knowledge conveyed by symbols."[27] Symbols take many forms including, story, myth, ritual, ceremony, icons, music, heroes, sheroes (patriarchally known as heroines), concepts, beliefs, artifacts, and art.[28] But symbols only work within the context that attaches meaning to them. They must be "attuned to people and place."[29] Symbols are powerful because they not only communicate information, they also elicit emotion; "they speak to both the mind and the heart."[30]

An example would be the symbol my interfaith student chaplains chose to represent their ministry on campus. They needed something that crossed the boundaries of all religions and finally chose a dove because of its intercultural significance as a symbol of peace—a symbol that spoke both to their minds and to their hearts. Use of a cross would have excluded the student chaplains who are not Christian, just as use of the Star of David would have excluded those who are not Jewish.

Not all symbols, of course, are as positive as the student chaplains' dove. The swastika, for example, has quite negative connotations as a reminder of the atrocities carried out in Germany under Adolf Hitler. The Confederate Flag, still considered a positive symbol of states' rights by some, has a decidedly threatening and deleterious connotation for anyone sensitive to racism and the domestic terrorism promulgated by the Ku Klux Klan.

Positively or negatively, human beings depend on symbol and metaphor to shape reality and to communicate alternative realities to one another. Bolman and Deal tell us we not only require symbols to communicate but that we take them for granted:

Symbols are the basic building blocks of the meaning systems, or cultures, that we inhabit. We live in cultures the same way that a fish lives in water. Just as fish are said to discover water last, our own cultural ways are often invisible to us.[31]

Primary symbolic communication tools are language and art. Language creates and reinforces reality.[32] According to Csikszentmihalyi, "The oldest symbolic systems in the world are those organized around content and the rules of language . . . perhaps only art, dance, and music are more ancient."[33] Even concepts like *worldviews, frames, domains,* and *conventional wisdom* are metaphors for helping us understand symbolically how the world works. Our ideas about God, our perceptions of one another, and our conceptions of reality are all symbol/metaphor dependent.

Metaphors and symbols help us to say the unsayable, to speak the unspeakable, to think the unthinkable. They are a means of expressing ideas, concepts, and feelings we cannot grasp in any other way. Sallie McFague says it well, " . . . the unfamiliar and inexpressible can only be imaged in the familiar and expressible."[34] Metaphors and symbols capture our attention as more literal language cannot. According to Bolman and Deal, "metaphors make the strange familiar and the familiar strange."[35]

In their discussions of metaphorical language for God, several authors point out that the power of a metaphor lies in its ability to make us ask not only how it is like but also how it is different from that to which it refers.[36] In fact, O'Day and Daw suggest that part of the problem in modern society with "Father" as a metaphor for God is that it no longer serves as a metaphor; somewhere in our history, we began to take this image literally.[37] (Getting students—and others—to use inclusive language for God is yet another adaptive challenge!)

In a multifaith context, it is particularly important to understand that no single image is adequate to represent the mystery of God. Images are finite; God is infinite.[38] Yet we use them nonetheless, because, inadequate as they are, metaphors are our only means of approaching the mystery, seeking some knowing of that which is unknowable. This is the power of metaphor, to point to that which is beyond the image itself,[39] and as Harris points out, "a mystery is not that about which we cannot know anything, but that about which we cannot know everything."[40]

One of the reasons metaphors are such a powerful aspect of language is because of the truth they contain. This is not factual truth, but truth in a much deeper sense, the sort of truth that Jesus meant when he said "You will know the truth, and the truth will make you free" (John 8:32). It is the sort of truth that poetry provides but, as Miller notes:

> "Poetry, mystery, and talk about revelation have more and more dropped out of contemporary life. . . . Biblical language might free us from some of these limitations if we were capable of thinking in such images, but we have become too literal in our thinking.[41]

Our literal thinking traps us in an "either/or" society, while our scriptures confront us with a need for a "both/and" understanding of God. An "either/or" understanding of God is definitely inadequate in a global context—and when our metaphors are inadequate, they cannot be true. The truth of any metaphor involves its adequacy to express the inexpressible.[42]

Many Christians have literalized their thinking about both God and the Bible, putting God in a Christian box, there to remain unsullied by all other approaches to the Divine. Some of my students are stunned each time I tell a class that *Allah* is simply the Arabic word for *God* and if they were living in an Arabic-speaking country the word they would use for *God* would be *Allah*, just as in a French-speaking country they would say *Dieu*, or in a German-speaking country they would say *Gott*. For many of my students, the metaphor contained in the word *God* has become literalized—and inadequate.

Coming to the realization that a metaphor is inadequate can be a very painful truth when that single metaphor has been the entire substance of one's paradigm. As Letty Russell notes, "Whenever one's paradigm or perspective on reality shifts, everything has to be thought through from this new perspective."[43] Paradigm shifts change the lens through which we perceive our existence. They can be epiphanies, offering us bright new insight into our being; they can result in theophanies, direct experiences of God; and they can destroy our old ways of thinking suddenly, painfully, and frighteningly.

Change is often profoundly difficult, particularly when something as fundamental as one's image of God or narrow religious worldview is at stake. The first time these fundamental symbols for making meaning are challenged can be particularly terrifying— and for students who have been raised with only one way of imagining God, becoming part of a multifaith environment on a college campus is often the first time such students have had to consider the possibility that their image of God is not the only one; that their truth is not the only truth. Because they have never so much as conceived the possibility that what they've been told all their lives might need to be examined, they have no experience with the possibility that faith questions can be survived. To use the metaphor coined by Richard Niebuhr, they realize their ship of faith is about to be wrecked upon the rocks of a new shore but they cannot imagine life in the new land even if they survive the shipwreck.[44] But to fail to change, to fail to grow, is to die in the present as we allow the past to strangle the future.[45]

Language, of course, is only one example of symbolic human communication. In the United States, we have become far more aware of religious and patriotic symbols since 9/11. Christian crosses have become more prevalent as jewelry and the American flag can be seen on the uniforms of sports teams, automobiles, jewelry, stationery, pens, pencils, and postage stamps. The flag is no longer just for the Fourth of July. "Especially in times of tragedies and triumphs, we embrace the spiritual magic symbols represent."[46]

Throughout human history, humans have attached symbolism to the way people dress and groups of people have been singled out for persecution because their manner of dress has made their difference visible. Following 9/11 anything Middle Eastern became threatening to the more xenophobic among us. On our campus, a professor from Pakistan (who is now a U.S. citizen) was advised by her husband to refrain from going out on the city streets in native costume. In Arizona, a Sikh man wearing a turban was murdered by an assailant who thought he was a Muslim.[47] Most of us understand that not all Muslims wear turbans. Many of us also know that not all persons who wear turbans are Muslim. But for the assailant, the turban had become a symbol of Islam, a religion the assailant had come to equate with terrorism. Ironically, despite the symbolism we humans attach to modes of dress, Islam is a religion which claims no physical symbols, equating their use with idolatry.[48]

Nonetheless, the ancient Sassamid emblem of the crescent moon has, over time, come to be associated with Islam,[49] just as for Judaism, a primary symbol is the Star of David. I was surprised to learn that, like the crescent moon for Islam, the association of the Star of David with Judaism is fairly recent. In ancient times, it was common in the Middle East and in North Africa as a symbol of good luck. In the seventeenth century it become fairly standard to place the Star of David on the exterior of synagogues, but it seems to have gained most of its recognition as a symbol of Judaism when it was adopted by the Zionist movement in 1897.[50]

Obviously the crescent moon, the Star of David, and the cross are identified uniquely enough with three of the world's great religions that seeing the symbols is sufficient to bring these religions to mind. I have found that these symbols can be useful during a retreat to facilitate discussion of their significance to adherents of the respective religions. Students seem to find it relatively nonthreatening to talk about symbols they all recognize and are fascinated by information about their origins as symbols for these religions. Through knowing something of their origins and meaning, students develop a framework for understanding the "other" while reinforcing their own faith. Parks notes that "faith develops at the boundary with otherness, when one becomes vulnerable to the consciousness of another, and thus vulnerable to reimagining self, other, world and 'God.'"[51]

Knitter understands that the very fate of the world may depend on interfaith dialogues. Noting that every religion has its claims for universal and normative truth, he reminds us of the importance of moving beyond these potential divisions "to work together for a more comprehensive justice, a deeper peace, and a more sustainable relationship with the ecosystem."[52]

Discussion of religious symbols usually leads to discoveries of other things Judaism, Christianity, and Islam have in common. For example, Muslims use prayer beads to recite the ninety-nine names of God.[53] These prayer beads are quite similar to the Rosary beads of Catholicism. Prayer shawls are found in both Judaism and Christianity. Beyond such physical symbols, all three religions share some basic stories with only minor differences, such as Adam and Eve in the Garden of Eden, and Abraham's banishment of Ishmael and Hagar.

Common ground is also to be found in a discussion of the attributes or character of God. Christians often turn to the fourth chapter of 1 John and suggest that "God is love" (1 John 4:8b). Jewish students speak of God's *chesed* (lovingkindness) and refer to texts in Exodus and the Psalms. Muslims note that God's foremost qualities are goodness, love, and compassion. "These are the attributes [of Allah] which the Qur'an and the Prophet refer to the most."[54]

Discussion of ethics, equality for all, and ideas of justice also build bridges that lead to common ground. Through such dialogues students of different faiths discover how much they share beneath the outer trappings of difference. Sometimes these discussions even transform difference from something to be feared and shunned into an invitation for exploration and discovery.

All three religions also have a deep commitment to hospitality for the stranger and they attach great importance to community. "Nothing is more central to most religious traditions than hospitality toward the neighbor, even toward the stranger."[55] The early church decided social and religious barriers were less important than community and "tore down the wall of separation between Jews and Gentiles."[56] In Islam, everything is done communally. "On a day to day level, Islam is a true religion of 'living together.'"[57]

Interfaith Experience and Shaping Community

One of the tenets of Bolman and Deal's symbolic frame is that "culture is the glue that holds an organization together and unites people around shared values and beliefs."[58] Were we to substitute the word *faith* in this statement in place of *culture* we would find this idea echoed by Sharon Parks who insists that "faith is a human universal that shapes both personal and corporate behavior."[59]

The word *faith* is itself a symbol loaded with meanings. Often it is equated with *belief* and *religion*, but Parks believes that faith is such an integral part of being human that it needs to be freed from the confines of being equated with religion so that it can be "reconnected with meaning, trust, and truth."[60] She is not referring to an exclusionary, we-have-the-only-right-answer sort of truth, but truth that understands God as the creator of all people everywhere, approached in different ways through different religions.

Parker Palmer reminds us that we come to know what we know in community with other people.[61] Thus, we come to know what we know of our faith within our faith community—and presumably the same would hold true of an interfaith community. One reason I offer interfaith retreats is precisely because community is important to our knowing. The retreats provide an environment of diversity in which people of different religions can come to know more about one another and each others' traditions. As one of my students noted following our winter retreat, "You cannot fully know someone until you know them spiritually, and you know what they believe and trust in" (see Appendix I).

Daniel Aleshire offers us the additional understanding that learning involves growth in our "capacity to live in relationship to the truth and to respond with obedience to that truth."[62] Change doesn't come easily, and worldviews/symbolic frames have to change before our view of reality can be transformed.[63] As new images emerge out of changing contexts and paradigms, old ways are threatened. However, if we make an effort to understand one another, we might not only gain insight into each other's viewpoints, but we might also begin to understand our own defensiveness when it comes to ideas which challenge our personal points of view.[64] When our perception of truth is so narrow and fragile that we cannot allow it to be challenged by another's perception, we effectively destroy community and deny ourselves the opportunity to grow, to be transformed.[65] "There is no point in meeting people from other communities of faith unless you want to grow in your relationship to God, and unless you are open to changing your behavior as a result."[66]

A primary means of shaping community at retreats is sharing meals together, keeping in mind the dietary restrictions of the faiths represented. Sharon Parks reminds us that human beings everywhere, in every culture have eaten together.[67] Sadly, that is not always the case for young adults these days. Raised in families stretched thin by working parents and an overabundance of after school activities, some of our students now come to college with little or no experience of community around a meal. For this reason, "there is a good deal at stake in whether or not mentoring communities incorporate a table practice as an elemental feature of common life."[68] While the dining hall offers the possibility for gathered community around a meal, the atmosphere is less rich and intimate than a meal students prepare and share together in a retreat setting. And, as previously noted, in the dining hall students tend to sit in groups of people most like themselves.

Making a Safe Transition

For many students, college marks their first real experience of being in close proximity to persons of other faiths. Both because of their encounters with religious "others" and because of the psychosocial developmental stage that comes with being a young adult away from home for the first time, they are comparing their ideas to those of others, examining their spiritual/religious beliefs and values, and searching for overall meaning in their lives.[69] While necessary to the development of a mature faith, as noted previously, the process of shifting paradigms can be frightening.

College chaplaincy involves hospitality and presence—making the campus a welcoming space for persons of all faiths and "being there" for students when the crises come (crises of faith, personal identity, a death in the family, or whatever else raises the specter of sudden and dramatic change). One of the ways to help students through the critical period of transition from adolescence to adulthood is to offer experiences that help them make sense of their shifting frames of reference. In my experience, interfaith retreats provide space for students to discover that "faithfulness to God involves openness to the wisdom of other religions as well as the treasures of our own faith."[70]

As noted at the beginning of this chapter, getting students to be open to the ideas of religions other than their own is an *adaptive challenge*. But failure to help today's young adults transition into patterns of thinking that embrace rather than exclude the religious "other" will stagnate their faith development and ultimately will threaten human existence, for "blinding ourselves to the text of someone else's life paves the path for us to hurt them."[71] No matter what faith tradition we claim as our own, if we insist that God is only accessible to people like us and only offers salvation to those who believe as we do, we have embraced an incredibly narrow-minded and selfish God. As Knitter suggests, "A loving God who loves only some people or who can overcome sinfulness and corruption in only some religions is somehow not a trustworthy God of love."[72] It is to an examination of this "trustworthy God of love" that we turn in chapter 3 through a comparison of three faith stories which constitute the bases of Judaism, Christianity, and Islam.

THREE

Vulnerability
The Divine Choice

Our ideas about God are shaped in numerous ways. Mine have grown out of my family of origin (Protestant mother and Catholic father), being raised in the Christian tradition, studying the Christian Bible, encounters with other religious traditions, my culture of origin (white, middle-class American), my gender, my love of nature, and the gift of a mind that has not been daunted by closed-minded religious authorities who tried to teach me that questioning and doubting were hazardous to religious well-being. The God in whom I was initially asked to believe and to whom I was expected to offer my worship was transcendent, omnipotent, omniscient, immutable, judgmental, punishing, impassible, invulnerable, and male. This God would send me to the eternal fires of hell unless I managed to convince *him* I was good enough to merit salvation which was somehow contingent upon my developing "a personal relationship with Jesus Christ."

This was problematic because the God to whom Jesus seemed to relate in the Gospels appeared to be very different from the God in whom I had been told I must believe. Even though questions and doubts were certain to keep me out of heaven, they kept forming in my mind. I spent a number of miserable years keeping my heretical thoughts to myself, yearning for a God I could love rather than fear. Eventually I left the church, but the longing (and my questions) remained.

Then in 1985, a friend invited me to sing with a small ensemble that performed at church dinners. I was leery, but figured dinners would be far enough removed from the practice of religion that the risk of a head-on collision with counterintuitive dogma was minimal. So I accepted my friend's invitation and began to experience a faithful community in which questions were both welcomed and encouraged. In their midst I was blessed to discover the God for whom I had longed, the God whom Jesus knew.

In this chapter I propose to explore this God: One who has a deep, passionate desire for mutual relationship with humankind which is profoundly revealed in God's chosen vulnerability, three primary examples of which are the Exodus of the Israelites from Egypt, the banishment of Hagar and Ishmael from the household of Abraham, and the cross/resurrection of Jesus Christ. As different as these three events may seem, I think they have a number of commonalities, which illuminate the nature of God as expressed in God's *chesed* (God's steadfast and enduring love). Significantly, each event was critical to the development of one of the world's monotheistic religions. The Exodus was the constitutive event of Judaism; it is through Ishmael that Muslims trace their ancestry to Abraham; the cross/resurrection was the defining event of Christianity.

God's *Chesed*

Through years of study and reflection, I have concluded that life is a risk God takes on us—again, and again, and again. Thankfully, God continues to find that risk worth taking—at least, God has so far. I believe the giving of life and its preservation are critical to the fulfillment of God's desire for relationship. God needs the creatures and the creation in order to be who God is. Artists have long known that a finished product is only the beginning of a larger creative process that cannot be completed until the creation enters into relationship.[1] My exploration of the three defining stories from Judaism, Christianity, and Islam will show that the gift of life is a gift of grace born of God's desire for relationship and that this gift is not dependent on human obedience but on God's *chesed.*

This aspect of God's character is spelled out in Exodus 34:6–7:

> The LORD, the LORD,
> a God merciful and gracious,
> slow to anger,
> and abounding in steadfast love and faithfulness,
> keeping steadfast love for the thousandth generation,
> forgiving iniquity and transgression and sin,
> yet by no means clearing the guilty . . .

In this text some of God's most basic characteristics are revealed. God is:

merciful and gracious
slow to anger
abounding in steadfast love and faithfulness
forgiving
justly judgmental

The text of Exodus 34:6–7 is echoed throughout the Old Testament[2] and these same characteristics of God are critical to the New Testament gospel. As was noted in chapter 2, God's goodness, love, and compassion, "are the attributes [of Allah] which the Qur'an and the Prophet refer to the most."[3]

The God described here is qualitatively different from the transcendent, omnipotent, omniscient, immutable, judgmental, punishing, impassible, invulnerable God on which I was raised. If God is merciful and gracious, God cannot be impassible. If God abounds in steadfast love and forgives iniquity, transgression, and sin, then God cannot be invulnerable. Love is impossible without risk (i.e., vulnerability). Forgiveness suggests that God is present with us, desiring relationship. Forgiveness would be pointless if God did not hope that a response would occur; that we would love God as God has loved us.[4] Furthermore, the judgmental, punishing God I was taught to fear was rather arbitrary and could be depended upon for judgment, but it would be judgment based on injured pride, jealousy, intolerance, and the prejudice that all humanity was entirely unworthy of its creator. The God described in Exodus 34 will not clear the guilty, but judgment will at least be just, based on steadfast love and full knowledge of all circumstances, and it will be tempered with understanding, mercy, and compassion.

Obviously, I write from a Christian perspective. But I am extremely cognizant of the multifaith environment in which I am called to proclaim the Gospel of Jesus Christ and our need, as followers of one who did not exclude anyone, to pay attention to the ways in which God's desire for relationship with humanity is revealed in faiths other than my own. I have chosen to include the Exodus in my exploration of God's vulnerability because I think we Christians too often lose sight of our Judaic roots. Christianity began as a sect of Judaism. We tend to forget that Jesus himself was a Mediterranean Jew, not a blond-haired, blue-eyed Anglo-Saxon Christian. I have chosen to use the story of Hagar and Ishmael's banishment because it reminds us that Muslims, like Christians and Jews, trace their origins back to Abraham.[5] Because of this common ancestry, "Muslims consider Jews and Christians their cousins as 'people of the Book.'"[6]

Our lack of understanding of other religions was painfully brought to my attention when I invited the members of my local ministerial alliance to participate in the multifaith memorial service on my campus on the first anniversary of September 11, 2001.[7] "I can't pray to *their* God," one pastor exclaimed vehemently; "I am not a Jew, or a Muslim, or a Hindu. I'm a Christian and I worship a Christian God." I had sudden flashbacks to the fearful God of my childhood and youth.

Had any of us at that meeting been born in another part of the world, in all likelihood we would have been raised as adherents of a non-Christian religion since only one-third of the world's population is Christian.[8] Certainly Jesus was not a Christian, yet he worshiped the same God we Christians profess. Surely God is the source of religious diversity in the world, drawing the human creature to the Divine Self in ways that are culturally meaningful over the course of human history. Religions that developed long before Judaism, Christianity, or Islam were conceived were as much a response of the human to the Divine as any of the newer religions. God, after all, is the source of all human inspiration. How arrogant we are when we put God in a box and demand that ours is the only appropriate way for humans to approach God and for God to respond to God's creation!

Including formative events of Judaism and Islam in this reflection on God's *chesed*, then, is partially motivated by my deep desire to break God free of the exclusionary self-righteousness I too often encounter in persons of my own faith. In our competitive society, we find it difficult to grasp what Henri Nouwen calls "the great spiritual mystery: to be chosen does not mean that others are rejected."[9]

Commonalities in Primary Stories from Three Faith Traditions

Human Needs: All three stories reveal humanity's need for deliverance and forgiveness. The Israelites need deliverance from Pharaoh's oppression (Exodus 5) and require forgiveness on a number of occasions during their journey to the promised land including the incident of their murmuring and recriminations shortly after they had begun their journey (Exodus 16:1–3), their disobedience in going out to gather bread on the Sabbath (Exodus 16: 27–28), and especially their idolatry with the golden calf (Exodus 32). If we define sin as that which interferes with relationship then surely Hagar was in need of forgiveness for her haughty attitude toward Sarah once Hagar became pregnant with Abraham's firstborn child and, like the Israelites, Hagar was in need of deliverance from slavery. These faith stories reflect to us who we are as human beings: the world is in need of deliverance and forgiveness, deliverance from the power of sin and forgiveness for continued disobedience to the will of God, particularly the new commandment Jesus gave, that we love one another (John 13:34). It is this deliverance and forgiveness Jesus came to offer the world (John 3:17).

Sin is that which disrupts our relationship with God, with one another, and with the rest of creation. When our image of God is so exclusionary that we are afraid to pray with a person of a different faith, that is sin. When our image of God is so self-righteous that we pray for God to convert persons of other faiths to Christianity, that is sin.[10] When our image of God is so limited that we can only pray for God to bless America rather than the world, that is sin. With the U.S. invasion of Iraq and the ever-increasing incidents of terrorism worldwide, we are poised on the brink of an abyss that could condemn the world to a hell far beyond our ability to imagine (for, if we could imagine it, surely we would redouble our efforts for peace). We are in desperate need of deliverance from the power of sin, some of which results from our individual choices and some of which has become systemic in our economics, our corporations, our governments, and even our religions.

Transformation: The Exodus, Hagar's story and the cross/resurrection transform the situation between humanity and God. What God chooses to do in each case may not make much sense by human standards: "For the message about the cross is foolishness to those who are perishing, but to us who are being saved it is the power of God" (1 Cor. 1:18). But God's love and wisdom go well beyond human comprehension:

> God chose what is foolish in the world to shame the wise; God chose what is weak in the world to shame the strong; God chose what is low and despised in the world, even things that are not, to bring to nothing things that are (1 Cor. 1:27–28).

God's loving-kindness (*chesed*) flowed through Jesus as he took everything sinful humanity could throw at him and said, "Father, forgive them; they don't know what they are doing" (Luke 23:34). "Forgive them and maintain your relationship with them." We should be amazed by the transformative nature of this great love.

We should also remember the context in which the story of Hagar appears, and be amazed at God's action. This was a patriarchal society in which women were considered to be property, valuable only because of their ability to bear children. As Sarah's slave, then, Hagar was the property of property; the only way she could have been more marginalized would be if she were as barren as Sarah. Yet God lifts Hagar up and gives heed to her affliction

(Genesis 16:11) and she eventually becomes the matriarch of an entire world religion through which God remains in relationship with over 20 percent of humanity in the modern world.[11]

God's continued forgiveness and redemption in the Exodus story are indicative of God's *chesed* and recurrent risk taking without which relationship with the Israelites would be lost. For me as a Christian, this story comes to its ultimate climax in the crucifixion/resurrection of Jesus Christ, which restores God's relationship with the entire world.

In no way do I believe God required or desired blood sacrifice for the redemption of human sin. Perhaps my rational mind is getting in the way here, but if God would willingly scapegoat Jesus, then God could easily require the same from the rest of us. However, God tells us God does not want blood sacrifice:

> For you have no delight in sacrifice;
>   if I were to give a burnt offering,
>   you would not be pleased.
> The sacrifice acceptable to God is
>   a broken spirit;
>   a broken and contrite heart,
>   O God, you will not despise (Psalm 51:16–17).

> For I desire steadfast love and not sacrifice,
> the knowledge of God rather than burnt offerings (Hosea 6:6).

God does have requirements for us—that we "do justice, love kindness, and walk humbly with our God" (Micah 6:8), but I believe the suffering of the cross was a risk God was willing to take because of God's *chesed* and deep desire for relationship with humanity. The cross was not a goal, but a consequence of God's love. God is willing to suffer to be in communion with us, and because God suffers with us, God understands our suffering. But, as the Giver of Life, one of God's goals surely must be the reduction of suffering in the world. How could love intentionally mete out suffering?

The Gospel of John boldly claims that "God *is* love" (1 John 4:8, 16), and in order to love us, God must be vulnerable to us and suffer with us, because love is impossible without vulnerability and openness to the risk of rejection, suffering, and loss. But the impossibility of loving without risking suffering does not make suffering a requirement; rather, it is a risk factor inherent in loving. This God who chooses to be in relationship with us gives us the freedom to return love for love—and suffers when we do not. "God suffers because God is vulnerable, and God is vulnerable because God loves—and it is love, not suffering or even vulnerability that is finally the point."[12]

When I reflect on John's statement "God is love," I wrestle with love being an attribute of God or God's very nature. If it is God's nature to love, then God really has no choice about loving. Yet the freedom to choose is what makes the gift of love meaningful. I think, for example, that Jesus had a choice about going to the cross; I do not think it was *obedience* to the *will* of God that took him there. Rather, it was his deep compassion for the world and his mutually loving relationship with God that gave him the courage to suffer and die on the cross. Carter Heyward feels that "*obedience* is a misleading metaphor. It suggests that God is a power *over* us more than a Spirit *with* us; that God speaks *down* to us more than God yearns for our companionship; and that God needs *obedient children* more than friends."[13]

I have long understood that without the freedom to choose, our love for God would be meaningless. But as I write this chapter, I realize that God must have that choice too. God's choice to be vulnerable in order to be in relationship with us is a function of God's free choice to be loving.

But if God has a choice, God could choose *not* to love us. In fact, the authors of Genesis tell us that God got so irritated with God's human creatures at one time that God loosed a great flood upon the earth (Genesis 7–8) to destroy what God had wrought, sorry that God had ever made humankind. But, in God's deep desire for relationship, not even God could give it all up. God saved Noah, his family, and two creatures of every kind. Then, in a sheer act of grace, God made a covenant never to let the waters of the great deep cover the earth again. The creation will continue, not because we deserve it, but because of God's great love, freely chosen.

This is a transforming, life-giving, relationship-building love and whenever God's life-giving, creation-continuing purposes get derailed, God acts to restore the Divine relationship with God's people. God makes promises and covenants that transform the human-Divine relationship into one of reciprocity and mutuality. The covenant God made with the Israelites at Mt. Sinai during the Exodus is a core story of Judaism. The promise God made to Hagar at the well called Beer-lahai-roi, that "I will so greatly multiply your offspring that they cannot be counted for multitude" (Gen. 16:10), is a core story of Islam. The covenant God made with the world through Jesus Christ is the core message of Christianity.

Revelation: God is the protagonist in all three events. God is not just behind the events like some *deus ex machina*, but integrally involved as the main character. These events are about God and who God is. Hagar and her unborn child would surely have died in the wilderness had God not appeared to her and told her to return to Sarah (Genesis 16:9). The astounding nature of God's direct intervention in her life is revealed in Hagar's reaction: "Have I really seen God and remained alive after seeing him?" (Genesis 16:13).

In the Exodus story we find God taking on Pharaoh in a power struggle over the Israelites. The issue at hand is who is sovereign, Pharaoh or God? Ironically, it is the Pharaoh himself who poses the question: "But Pharaoh said, 'Who is the LORD, that I should heed him and let Israel go?'" (Exodus 5:2a).

Of course, ultimately this is the question answered by the entire Bible: Who is God? And time and again, we are surprised by the answer. In fact, we are stunned by the incomprehensible nature of God's *chesed*—a steadfast love that is not dependent on human obedience, a steadfast love that takes risks for the sake of relationship, a steadfast love that continually turns human expectations upside down, a steadfast love that died on a cross rather than let go of sinful humanity.

Indeed, rarely will anyone die for a righteous person—though perhaps for a good person someone might actually dare to die. But God proves his love for us in that while we still were sinners Christ died for us (Romans 5:7–8).

These stories reveal the character of God who is willing to risk a broken heart to bring salvation to God's people. This is a God who *chooses* to keep covenant with humanity. This is a God who is "merciful and gracious, slow to anger and abounding in steadfast love and faithfulness" (Exodus 34:6), despite the grief and suffering in which such love inevitably results.

Power: The Pharaoh rules with a hammering fist; God rules with a vulnerable open hand.[14] God's hand is open because God does not coerce. In fact, God shares power with humanity, for to be in meaningful relationship with human beings, God must share power. If humans did not have freewill—the power to make decisions and choices, including the choice of loving God—we would be back to the situation already noted, that any human feelings for God would be required and, consequently, devoid of meaning. As Anthony DeMello notes, "Love can only exist in freedom."[15]

From the very beginning God chose to share power, giving dominion to the human creature (Gen. 1:26–30). God shared power with Abraham by consulting him about the fate of Sodom and Gomorrah and taking Abraham's opinion seriously (Genesis 18:16–33). God shared power with Moses when God listened to Moses' argument against Divine destruction of the Israelites over the golden calf episode (Exodus 32:11–14). This also reveals that God is not immutable, for God not only listened to Moses, God changed God's mind. God repeatedly shares power, working through humans to accomplish Divine purposes: kings and prophets, Hagar and Hannah, the disciples, the Apostle Paul, Mary the mother of Jesus, and of course, Jesus himself. Nor did God stop sharing Divine power when the biblical canon was closed. God continues to work through people to bring about the kingdom of God on earth. God surely worked through Martin Luther King, Jr., Mother Theresa, Mahatma Gandhi, and Dag Hammerskjold to name but a few more contemporary examples. God works through each of us whenever we manage to have compassion for one another (Matthew 25:40).

The ultimate significance of these stories is that they show us what God is like against all expectations; they shock us into new understanding of the Divine. The cross particularly shows what God intends sovereignty to be, what power is all about. It is a concept that turns traditional human understandings of power entirely upside down and gives us a new kind of power.[16] "Jesus transforms the love of power into the power of love."[17]

Because God chooses, from the beginning, to share power with humanity, the possibility exists from the very beginning that the Divine will may not be done. Here again, God takes a risk. But, as noted previously, God's power would be meaningless if there were no other beings with at least some degree of power who could choose to interact with God.

Vulnerability: Toward the beginning of this chapter I stated that God is One who has a deep, passionate desire for mutual relationship with humankind which is profoundly revealed in God's chosen vulnerability. True power is vulnerable; vulnerability, unlike weakness, is a choice made from a position of strength. The ultimate strength is to choose to be vulnerable, but one must be strong before one can choose. God's choice of vulnerability in God's relationship to humanity reveals the strength of God's power.

Vulnerability as strength is counterintuitive in a culture that thrives on "might makes right" and finds weakness abhorrent. We want (need?) God to be "almighty." When I suggest to my students that God shares power and that vulnerability is a primary characteristic of the Divine, they are often both shocked and dismayed. Even some of my seminary professors have reacted to this idea with outrage; in a culture that holds rugged individualism as a primary virtue, the idea that one of God's most basic characteristics is vulnerability is downright menacing. Invulnerability has become a cultural idol.

If God is vulnerable, then God can suffer. This is unacceptable in a society that believes suffering should not exist at all. Barbara Brown Taylor suggests this attitude is partly due to incredible technological advances that have allowed us to relieve suffering in ways unheard of a few short years ago.[18] But when we run away from suffering we actually make things worse. Suffering spreads when we turn our backs on it. "When we ignore suffering in those with whom we live, we cut ourselves off from kinship with them. When we deny it in ourselves, we become numb to the deep parts of ourselves where both joy and sorrow live. Or worse."[19] When we ignore God's suffering or find Divine suffering inconceivable, we deny ourselves and God the incredible blessing of relationship; we fail to know the deep joy of a Divine friend who willingly walks with us through our deepest sorrows and longs to help us carry the burdens heaped on by life's messiness.

Our abhorrence of suffering and our aversion to vulnerability are two major reasons we find so unacceptable the image of a vulnerable God who can be grievously wounded by human sin. Thus the common image of God in our culture, even for people who do not "believe in" God, is one of a powerful being who dominates *his* creatures, even using violence if necessary. Humans, created in the image of God, are surely justified then in using violence to achieve personal, corporate, and national greatness. These attitudes are indicative of the depth of our fear of being vulnerable. "Probe violence and the quest for domination far enough, and one always finds the fear of weakness."[20]

In 2 Corinthians 12, Paul boasts of his weaknesses, finally saying that to keep him humble he was given a "thorn in the flesh" which three times he asked Christ to remove. But Jesus said, "My grace is sufficient for you, for power is made perfect in weakness" (2 Cor. 12:9a). Undergirded by Jesus' words, Paul wrote to the Corinthians:

> So I will boast all the more gladly of my weaknesses, so that the power of Christ may dwell in me. Therefore I am content with weaknesses, insults, hardships, persecutions, and calamities for the sake of Christ; for whenever I am weak, then I am strong" (2 Corinthians 12:9–10).

God continually risks rejection, suffering, and loss. Love allows itself to be wounded. "Invulnerable love" would be a fundamental contradiction. God is strong because God is vulnerable. "Only a sovereign God can choose divine vulnerability."[21]

Mutability: Another implication of power sharing is that God must adapt God's actions according to circumstance; God is not simply active, but reactive. God's salvific will does not change; God's *chesed* does not change. ". . . his steadfast love endures forever"

(Psalm 136). "As the Father has loved me, so I have loved you; abide in my love" (John 15:9).

I believe God has a specific, live-giving, love-incarnating purpose for creation. Because of this, whenever the risk God takes on humanity goes awry, God must react in order to keep creation moving toward God's ultimate goal. This doesn't mean that God does not punish. The description of God in Exodus 34:6–7 reveals both God the steadfast lover and God the just disciplinarian. The tension here arises from God's *chesed*. In the face of human disobedience, God's grace, mercy, and steadfast love mean the story will be one of the triumph of grace, but not without cost to both humanity and to God for human disobedience. However, God's *chesed* is so strong that God is willing to bear this cost.

Throughout the Bible, God changes God's mind in order to keep the story going. Sometimes in response to prayer for one's own well-being, sometimes in response to the plea of an intercessor, sometimes with no human mediation at all (because God realizes God must change in order to be who God is), God reverses what God said God would do or what God has already started doing, because God's loving-kindness is stronger than God's anger.[22] A God who chooses to be vulnerable must be open to being moved and changed by circumstances.

McCann suggests that God's change of mind about destroying the Israelites after they made the golden calf "may even surpass the significance of the Exodus, because God clearly knows what kind of people he is choosing to save."[23] God, clearly knew when Jesus died, too:

> And when they had taken their places and were eating, Jesus said, "Truly I tell you, one of you will betray me, one who is eating with me" (Mark 14:18).

> While he was still speaking, suddenly a crowd came, and the one called Judas, one of the twelve, was leading them. He approached Jesus to kiss him; but Jesus said to him, "Judas, is it with a kiss that you are betraying the Son of Man?" (Luke 22:47–48).

But Peter said, "Man, I do not know what you are talking about!" At that moment, while he was still speaking, the cock crowed. The Lord turned and looked at Peter. Then Peter remembered the word of the Lord, how he had said to him, "Before the cock crows today, you will deny me three times." And he went out and wept bitterly (Luke 22:60–62).

God knows us and still desires relationship with us. Yet God does not ignore the guilty. Our actions have consequences and human failure to return love for love has a price: Peter wept; Judas couldn't live with the guilt (Matthew 27:3–5). These were Jesus' closest friends. And, though love does not count the cost, a price was paid: Jesus died.

Grace: The three faith stories under discussion affirm that God's grace/deliverance/salvation is not dependent on human obedience. Rather, human obedience is a response to God, a thanksgiving for deliverance and a means of maintaining relationship with God. That is, human obedience to what God desires (that we "do justice, love kindness, and walk humbly with our God") is not a coerced response to an authoritarian God but an attitude of gratitude toward a God whose love can break hearts of stone "and give us hearts for love alone."[24]

Salvation comes before repentance. We are saved by Grace. God brought the people out of Egypt (Exodus 12, ff.) before the law was given to Moses on Mt. Sinai (Exodus 20). In his letter to the Romans, Paul argues that this same relationship between grace and the law is operative in Christ's death; that grace is not dependent on obedience to the law. Paul says that the salvific nature of the crucifixion supersedes salvation brought about through the keeping of ritual law.[25] "For Christ is the end of the law so that there may be righteousness for everyone who believes" (Romans 10:4).

This understanding surely comes out of Paul's own personal experience on the Damascus Road when he, still Saul of Tarsus, heard God's suffering through the voice of Christ and experienced God's love and transforming grace for him, a Roman Jew intent on persecution of heretical Jews who were claiming Jesus as the Messiah (Acts 9). Because of our sinfulness, the communion that is God's ultimate aim for human life "is possible only through justification and grace."[26]

Yet, my students are startled by the idea of grace. They have been indoctrinated with the conventional wisdom that understands Christianity as a system of requirements and rewards that is about believing the right things rather than being about developing a mutual loving relationship with God. That is, of course, the Christianity I too once knew, under the thumb of God-the-Enforcer. My students are awed to discover a God who loves them just as they are. A new hope for organized religion is sometimes sparked in them by the possibility that Christianity is not about right beliefs and impossible standards but about life-giving relationships with God, Jesus, and the faith community.

We Christians are fortunate that the story of Hagar and Ishmael has come down to us in the Scripture we hold as sacred and we would do well to heed the message underlying the fact that God heeded the cry of an Egyptian slave in a Hebrew household. "The compassion shown by the God of Israel for Hagar the Egyptian reveals that God's salvific purposes know neither ethnic nor gender boundaries."[27] Obviously, I believe they know no religious boundaries either.

Of course, at any point of human sin, the relationship between God and humanity suffers and could be permanently broken; God could choose to end the story. But God does not, because "God does not deal with us according to our sins, nor requite us according to our iniquities" (Psalm 103:10). As McCann has noted:

> Israel's disobedience in Exodus 32:1–14 was not the end of the story. Peter's denial and the disciple's unfaithfulness were not the end of the story. The church's history of disobedience has not ended the story of God's dealing with a chosen people. The church is saved by grace![28]

As a Christian, I believe the cross is the ultimate act of grace in which God demonstrates how far God is willing to go.

Relationship: In Genesis 16, Hagar is saved from the wilderness that she might live to give birth to Ishmael who will become the ancestor to Islam. In Genesis 21, God saves Hagar and Ishmael from dying of thirst in the wilderness by showing Hagar a spring at which she then fills her water bag and brings water to Ishmael.

According to Muslim historiography, when Hagar and Ishmael reached the Ka'ba they were out of water. Hagar was desperate to ensure Ishmael's survival and ran in search of water between Safa and Marwa, two small hills next to the Ka'ba. Allah caused a spring to gush up in front of her near the path around the Ka'ba.[29] Here in the twenty-first century, during the Hadj, "after pilgrims have circumambulated the Ka'ba, they trot, with shoulders shaking, seven times between two low hills in imitation of the frantic Hagar searching in despair for water for wailing little Ishmael."[30] Muslims reenact this part of the story as a means of remembering God's saving act. This event is fundamental to Muslim understanding of the Divine-human relationship. And what is the point of practicing any religion if not to maintain relationship with the Divine?

Instructions for maintaining the relationship between God and the people of God are part of both the Exodus story and the cross/resurrection story. As noted above, God delivers the law to Moses in the midst of the Exodus to the Promised Land. The Israelites are freed from Egypt. But freedom is never just "from"; freedom is also "for." In this case, the Israelites were freed *for* the service of God through the covenant made at Sinai. The intent of the law is to engender life. "You shall keep my statutes and my ordinances; by doing so one shall live; I am the LORD" (Leviticus 18:5).

In the cross/resurrection event, Jesus brought freedom *from* the power of sin *for* the service of God. We also have the assurance that Jesus is with us always (Matthew 28:20). His continued presence maintains the Divine-human relationship—God's deep and passionate desire, profoundly revealed in God's chosen vulnerability. The human response to this Divine act of saving grace is to be one of loving service: "Simon, son of John, do you love me? . . . Feed my sheep" (John 21:17).

Before Jesus' birth, Mary was told she would bear a son who should be called Emmanuel, which means *God with us* (Matthew 1:23). "What we see in the incarnation is not the human effort to reach the Divine, but the Divine reaching out for us—and through no merits of our own, we are included"[31] because God is unwilling to be alone and unwilling for us to be alone, as the sacred texts of Judaism, Christianity, and Islam bear witness:

"You hunt me like a lion" (Job 10:16).

"The voice of the Lord cries to the city" (Micah 6:9).

"Where are you, Adam?" (Genesis 3:9).

Know that I am with you and will keep you wherever you go . . ." (Genesis 28:15a).

Be strong and courageous; do not be frightened or dismayed, for the LORD
your God is with you wherever you go (Joshua 1:9b).

. . . in every place where I cause my name to be remembered, I will come to you and bless you (Exodus 20:24b).

And I will ask the Father, and he will give you another Advocate, to be with you forever (John 14:16).

I will not leave you orphaned; I am coming to you (John 14:18).

And remember, I am with you always, to the end of the age (Matthew 28:20b).

We indeed created man; and We know what his soul whispers within him, and
We are nearer to him than the jugular vein (Qur'an 50.16).

We know in our hearts, if not in our heads, that we need God. But the idea that God needs us is mind-boggling. This is the relationship that Martin Buber so exquisitely explored in his book *Ich and Du*.[32] We are God's beloved every bit as much as Jesus was and that means that God desires a mutually loving relationship with us. "Mutuality and relationship belong to the eternal dynamics of love."[33] And because mutuality is such a part of the Divine-human relationship, God asks us "Do you love me?" and then offers us countless chances to say "Yes" (John 21:15–17). God is a relational God and we, created in God's image, are relational beings. As I discussed in chapters 1 and 2, we need relationships to be whole. We cannot be human alone.

Yet we struggle with stories of God's desire for us because we would much prefer to have God on our terms rather than God's terms. In fact, one of the greater sins of Christendom, I think, has been to re-create God in our own image.[34] But we are blessed to have the God we need rather than the one we would box into religious requirements, "right" beliefs, and earned grace. Of course, Jesus ended up on the cross because he was not the God we expected; he was not the God we wanted on our terms.[35]

Cosmic Effect of Salvation: Salvation is not limited; it is a universal, world-encompassing act of God. "In Christ God was reconciling the *world* to himself" (2 Cor. 5:19). In all three faith stories considered in this chapter, God is publicly expressing God's passion for life, justice, peace, and relationship with *all* of creation. These events happened right in the midst of the messiness of daily human life. Their public and countercultural nature reveals their cosmic scope, God acting in the world for all the world, so all the world could know. But all the world does not know, for all the world is neither entirely Jewish, nor entirely Muslim, nor entirely Christian and these are faith stories of specific religious traditions.

The only way we can offer proof of these stories' truths to the world is to live them. That is the risk of faith. The proof of a paradigm's truth lies in its being lived. The Old Testament is the way Israel lived; the New Testament is the way the early church lived; the Qur'an is the revelation of how Muslims are to live. The living of these stories proves their truth for these communities of faith.

This tempts me to ask what truths we are living in our communities of faith here in the early twenty-first century. Are the ancient stories still our stories, or have authoritarian dogma and patriarchal tradition corrupted the truth the ancients lived? The apparently heretical idea of God's vulnerability would suggest that the God most Christians "know" is an idolatrous perversion of the God revealed in scripture. Dennis, Sheila, and Matthew Linn *warn* us that "we become like the God we adore."[36] They feel we must heal our image of God if we are to live as God intended. In our age of religious pluralism, in a culture consumed by winner-take-all, might-makes-right, individualistic mentality, I believe it is of life-preserving importance for us to remember (i.e., piece back together) the vulnerable, relational, steadfastly loving God of these ancient faith stories.

Beyond Hagar and the Exodus

As Christianity emerged from its Jewish roots, it developed its own unique theological understandings, two of which further illuminate God's deep, passionate desire for mutual relationship with humankind and God's choice to risk vulnerability in order to fulfill God's desire. These are: 1) the Trinitarian nature of God and 2) Jesus as the unique and only means of salvation.

The Trinitarian Nature of God: The doctrine of the Trinity developed, of course, over time. What were Christians to do with the one true God who chose to reveal Godself in Jesus, who then promised to be present with humankind "to the end of the age" (Matthew 28:20b) through the Holy Spirit? How were Christians to remain monotheistic with a savior born in human flesh whose name, Emmanuel, meant "God with us?" (Isaiah 7:14; Matthew 1:23) If Jesus was the Divine Logos, the creative Word of God; if "the Word was God" (John 1:1) and "became flesh and lived among us" (John 1:14), then was Jesus God?

These and similar questions that arose from the biblical witness were resolved with the formation of the doctrine of the Trinity—that God is one, revealed in three persons: Father, Son, and Holy Spirit. This suggests that God, whose full mystery of being is beyond human comprehension, is by nature relational and risks relationship with creation by daring to create in the first place, and by loving the creation in life-sustaining ways, empowering the human creature to give and receive love just as God does. A Trinitarian "God is not about power and self-sufficiency and the assertion of authority but about mutuality and equality and love."[37] God is one who shares life, shares love, and shares power—within God's self and with what God creates. God's power is only realized in God's loving and mutuality, but years of Christian tradition have transformed the understanding of God's power as with us and among us to an authoritarian understanding of power over us. Part of this transgression[38] is surely a result of the patriarchy that was also developing in Christianity as power became concentrated in a male priesthood. If the doctrine of the Trinity had been formulated as Parent, Child, and Holy Spirit, perhaps Christian theology would have developed a more mutual, power-sharing understanding of who God is and we would not find the idea of God as vulnerable quite so startling.

I believe that our understanding of God directly influences how we live our lives, how we relate to one another, and how we relate to God. I think the God of authoritarian intractability developed in Christendom has been used for centuries to coerce people, to justify war, and to validate hierarchical, authoritarian structures in the church, in the family, and in society at large. Made afraid of God's vengeance, we have confused God's power with God's love. I believe much of Christianity desperately needs to heal its image of God in order to truly understand the relational, mutual, vulnerable communion revealed by a Trinitarian understanding of God.

Jesus as the Unique Means of Salvation: Since I have already discussed the cosmic effect of salvation, my position should be clear: God's salvation is not limited. But, is Jesus the only means by which salvation is achieved?

As a Christian, the life, death, and resurrection of Jesus are, for me, the definitive revelation of who God is—one who has a deep, passionate desire for mutual relationship with humankind. Growing up with an idea of God as one who could, and would, destroy me without warning if I did not believe in Jesus, I felt very fortunate to have been born into a Christian family. I was terribly afraid of God, but clung to Jesus for salvation from God's wrath. I was so focused on the second half of John 3:16, "that whosoever believed in him [Jesus] would not perish but would have eternal life," that I did not question the doctrine of Jesus as the sole means of salvation.

But, as I met people of other faiths, as I developed friendships with Jews, Buddhists, Sikhs, Muslims, and Hindus, I worried about the fate of their souls when they died—and, having by this time discovered a God who is love, I began to question how God could love the entire world and yet predestine non-Christians to eternal damnation. It seemed to me that by sending Jesus, God was only saving the part of the world that managed to know about Jesus; that God was somehow creating a salvation system of "haves" and "have nots." Was this something love would do?

In my wrestling, I eventually discovered John 3:17: "Indeed, God did not send the Son into the world to condemn the world, but in order that the world might be saved through him." If God wanted to save the world, why would God create a system of salvation which would only save the portion that believed in Jesus?

Going back to John 3:16, and reading John 14:6,[39] it was obvious that Jesus was the unique means of salvation. Or was it? Did *him* in "whosoever believed in *him*" refer to Jesus or to God? Did Jesus mean belief in him was the only way to salvation ("No one comes to the Father except through me"—John 14:6), or, answering Thomas's question about how to find where Jesus was going, did Jesus mean, "I have shown you the way; *I Am* [God] is the way;[40] live in mutual relation with each other; 'love one another as I have loved you' (John 15:12)?" *God* is the source of human salvation and whatever means we have of being in relationship with God—including "other" faiths—must be valid or God would have to give up on two-thirds of the world; if God can condemn "them," what is to keep God from deciding to condemn "us" as well? If that thought is not radical enough, I would point out that if one must be Christian to achieve salvation then Jesus is doomed; he was a Jew.

Jesus did not come to condemn the world (John 3:17). Yet we Christians have condemned much of it in Jesus' name. We have forced our religion on people who led deeply spiritual lives in communion with God through other religions (e.g., Native Americans). One prominent Protestant denomination has been in the news as its members have mounted campaigns to pray for the conversion (to Christianity) of Jews and Muslims.

As Christians, we know God through Jesus Christ, but are we not rather arrogant to insist that the rest of the world must see God in the same way? Is God's grace something to be earned through belief in Jesus or is it a Divine gift, freely given that God does not limit to those who believe "rightly?" Is the doctrine of Jesus as the unique means of salvation universally true, or is it only true for a religion that seeks power, authority, and supremacy over others? Has Christianity stopped serving the purpose for which it was intended—to bring the good news of God's love to the world, as revealed in Jesus Christ? Has Christianity become idolatrous?

Carl Braaten says, "Christian theology cannot relinquish the claim of eschatological finality in connection with the historical figure of Jesus without surrendering the ground principle of Christian identity."[41] But has our understanding of Jesus' eschatological finality become exclusionary in a way that God never intended? If we believe that God is definitively revealed in Jesus, how can we believe God is going to exclude anyone; did Jesus? If God deeply and passionately desires mutual relationship with *all* of humankind, and not just with Christians, then the God who loves enough to become incarnate in order to be with us, who shares power in order to receive as well as to give love, who risks being hurt in order to stay in relationship with us, will not exclude anyone from the salvation brought to *the world* in Jesus Christ. It is a profound mystery to me how we as Christians can believe that God is love and then try to limit that love to those who believe as we do. I continue to be struck by the revealing statement a Jewish rabbi made to Joseph DiNoia: "Jesus Christ is the answer to a question I have never asked."[42]

As Christians I think we are arrogant to limit God and the salvation of creation to *our* doctrines, *our* beliefs, *our* scriptures, and *our* questions. I believe our need to "be right" reveals our profound fear of a God who is not love but authoritarian power. I do not believe a God of love would hinge our salvation on being right. Rather, we are saved by God's *chesed*, God's loving-kindness, God's deep desire for mutual relationship with those whom God will never let go, a God who showed us just how far that love will go in Jesus Christ.

I have a profound love of Jesus and the God I know through him. I would have others know Jesus too, not because their eternal salvation depends on it, but because I would share the joy of this friendship and life-giving way of living. If I am to share my love of Jesus with those who are not Christian, then I must be willing to listen to the joys they find in their religions as well. Otherwise I am denying the mutuality of relationship that I believe is among God's deepest desires for humankind. Jesus is the way to salvation for the world in the sense that if we all embodied his community-building mutuality, his power-sharing authority, and his nonexclusionary love, then swords would be beaten into ploughshares and we would, at last, know the kingdom of God on earth. The salvation Jesus offers is for the survival of creation itself—a creation loved beyond our wildest imaginings by a God who passionately desires mutual relationship with the world and all that dwell herein.

God Is with Us

Each February with the approach of Lent, I think of the forty days Jesus spent in the desert wilderness, tempted by Satan but with angels to guard and guide him. God was there too. I think of the two times Hagar went to the wilderness, first to flee Sarah's anger and subsequently because Sarah banished her. God was with her both times, saving her from certain death. I think of the Israelites wandering in the desert wilderness for forty years; God was with them, guiding them, feeding them, and providing water for them. I think of the wilderness wanderings we face because our country's leaders led us into war, in another desert—and I know God is there too.

God is with us wherever we go (Joshua 1:9), in all that we do, sometimes wounded by us, suffering with us when we are wounded, rejoicing with us when we live as God created us to live, loving our neighbors as God has loved us. Choosing to be vulnerable, loving us and desiring our love, God is with us "especially in the wilderness, because he has been in the wilderness with us. He has been in the wilderness for us. He has been acquainted with our grief and loving him we will come at last to love each other too."[43] Who but God could have made such a Divine choice?

FOUR

Created to Relate and to Create

*Then God said, "Let us make humankind in our image,
according to our likeness; and let them have dominion over
the fish of the sea, and over the birds of the air, and over
the cattle, and over all the wild animals of the earth, and
over every creeping thing that creeps upon the earth." So
God created humankind in his image, in the image of God
he created them; male and female he created them.*

—Genesis 1:26–27 (NRSV)

What does it mean to be created in the image of God? This question has been a topic of discussion for centuries. The only place in the Bible that this language occurs is in Genesis, chapters 1 through 11, though it is implied in Psalm 8.[1] I think the image one holds of God directly affects one's interpretation of what it means to be made in God's image.

Those who would define God as the World Intellect define the "image" as intellect; those who would define God as "love" locate the image in the human capacity to love; those who would define God as process or relationship define the image in the same way. Whatever God is, as God's image, humans share in the divine.[2]

Relationship and Responsibility

As should be obvious from chapter 3, it is my belief that God created the world and all that lies herein, including we human creatures, out of a deep desire for relationship. Furthermore, a basic premise of chapter 1 is that the primary purpose of being human is to be in relationship with God. God is a relational being. Those of us who are Trinitarian in our theology experience God as a mystery whose self-expression is the epitome of relationship: community, three in one—Creator, Redeemer, and Comforter.[3] The third "person" of God, the Holy Spirit, the Comforter Jesus said God would send—the Advocate or Helper (John 14:25)—is also the source of our inspiration, *inspiration* and *spirit* coming from the same root word meaning breath or wind; *to inspire* literally means *to breathe in.* God is the breath of life itself and the source of our imagination.

I think a key to understanding the language of Genesis is the concept of relationship. Created in God's image, we reflect who God is to the rest of creation. Moltmann tells us that "to be an image of something always means letting that something appear, and revealing it."[4] Consequently, at least in part, being created in the image of God means that we reveal something of God to one another. Being in relationship with other persons, we learn something of what it means to be in relationship with God.[5] The Qur'an indicates that humanity was created as God's viceregent on earth; thus we are God's agents to the rest of creation.[6] All of this suggests that we are created to be friends with God and to be the instruments of God's caring for creation. This is reflected in the language of Genesis 1:28–30 which indicates humanity is to "have dominion over" the rest of creation. Sadly, instead of taking this to mean we are to be responsible stewards caring for the earth, too many of us have taken *dominion* to mean *domination* and have even used these verses as an excuse for exploitation of the earth's resources.

Though God has given us the gift of free will, it does not come without responsibility. The choices we make and the actions we take would surely give us pause if we truly paid attention to being the representatives of God on earth, called to care for and protect its resources rather than exploit them. Created in the image of God, we are responsible to God for our choices and the actions that result from them.[7] Creation is an ongoing process[8] in which God calls us to be cocreators in the actions necessary for repair of the world (*tikkun olam* in the Jewish tradition[9]). "In our freedom to choose, God gives us the blessing of empowerment and creativity. In our ability to choose, God calls us to be partners and co-creators."[10] In this chapter I shall explore human creativity as a pathway to fulfillment of our primary human purpose, relationship with God.

Humans Are Creative Beings

When God created humans in God's own image, God made a choice not to be the only one in the universe with creative power. "In spite of the risks involved, God chose the way of less than absolute control for the sake of a relationship of integrity in which power is shared with that which is other than God."[11] In so doing, God left the future open to a variety of possibilities.[12]

God created us with minds capable of innovation and imagination, that is, creativity—a divine gift that needs to be encouraged if we are to fulfill our role as cocreators. It is our creativity that leads us to experience wonder, mystery, awe, and even ecstasy. These sorts of experiences are undervalued in our culture yet I believe they are vital to the development of our awareness of the Divine. Religious experiences are born in the creative imagination and may or may not eventually be understood by the rational intellect.[13] "Creativity comes through an openness toward the mystery of God and a recognition that emotion as well as intellect, desire as well as duty, must be a part of one's relationship to God."[14] Humans are not only rational beings; we are also aesthetic beings.

In 1996, Oxford zoologist Alister Hardy suggested that an awareness that leads to religious experience is a natural part of being human. He thinks that this capacity for awareness of the

Divine Other has been hardwired into our biology because it helps us survive.[15] If one accepts Hardy's theory, then even persons who are nontheists have an innate attraction to the realm of mystery and wonder which offers the possibility of relationship to the Other, however the Other is conceived.[16] Epperly and Solomon remind us that "the Divine imprint is our deepest reality. We bear the reflection of God in every thought, word, and deed."[17] Out of a desire to connect with the Divine, "to make the sacred a reality in our daily lives,"[18] humans engage in sacred rituals and spiritual practices.

Ritual and Traditional Spiritual Practices

What is a ritual? Why are rituals important? What elements of ritual are common across religions? How are rituals influenced by or derived from culture? What is a spiritual practice and why do humans bother with such activities? How does culture influence spiritual practice? What are spiritual disciplines? What role does imagination play in spiritual development and practice? These are among the many questions that can surface as we intentionally think about ritual and spiritual practice. Our lives are bound in habitual acts and routines we perform every day almost without thinking about them that seem to anchor our sense of well-being, such as starting the day with a cup of coffee and brushing our teeth before going to bed. When these actions offer us experience that seems set apart from ordinary time, they become rituals.

We often mark the important moments in our lives with rituals thereby acknowledging their particular significance. Examples would be commencement rites, wedding ceremonies, rituals surrounding the birth of a child, cultural ceremonies performed at puberty, etc. In North American culture, sporting events, particularly football, have taken on a ritual aspect with weekly performances culminating in championship games. However, Rachel Pollock, while recognizing that such secular rituals certainly provide moments of experience outside ordinary time, suggests they do not "show us glimpses of a world beyond our ordinary experience. They do not address our yearning to touch the Divine and let it enter our lives."[19]

Sacred ritual and spiritual practices, on the other hand, open the heart to a realm of mystery and awe and create an inner awareness of the Divine.[20] They offer us the deeper experiences that give our lives meaning. These rituals often involve the retelling of familiar stories that bind us together in community with others, helping us make our individual stories part of the larger story of a faith tradition or culture. As the character August Boatwright notes in *The Secret Life of Bees*, "Stories have to be told or they die, and when they die, we can't remember who we are or why we're here."[21]

Examples of rituals that are intertwined with the retelling or remembering of sacred stories include the recitation of the story of the Israelites liberation from Egypt during the Passover meal and the reenactment of Hagar's search for water during the Hadj. All of the world's religions include rituals and spiritual practices that help to open a path between the world of our everyday experience and the mysterious, invisible realm of the sacred, doorways to the Divine known to the ancient Celts as "thin places."[22]

One virtually universal spiritual practice found in all religions is prayer. In some, kneeling and prostration are a necessary part of prayer; other religions do not permit kneeling. For example, "rabbinic law expressly forbids kneeling at any time except during one specific prayer on Yom Kippur."[23] But whatever form it takes, prayer is a primary means for humans to enter into and nurture a relationship with God.[24] My students, regardless of their faith tradition, seem particularly appreciative of the description of prayer offered by Walter Wink:

> Praying is rattling God's cage and waking God up and setting God free and giving this famished God water and this starved God food and cutting the ropes off God's hands and the manacles off God's feet and washing the caked sweat from God's eyes and then watching God swell with life and vitality and energy and following God wherever God goes.
>
> When we pray, we are not sending a letter to a celestial White House, where it is sorted among piles of others. We are engaged, rather, in an act of co-creation, in which one little sector of the universe rises up and becomes translucent,

incandescent, a vibratory center of power that radiates the power of the universe.[25]

Other traditional spiritual practices found in many religions include meditation, fasting, silence, study, and corporate worship. In the Christian tradition, some would add journaling as a spiritual practice. "Journal writing tends to draw insights and feelings from us that may otherwise be missed. In the process of writing, we often come to greater consciousness, clarity, and perspective."[26]

Spiritual practices help us to focus our questioning and seeking as we develop a relationship with the Divine. "It is possible to speak of spirituality as a universal human activity because life is filled with experiences that drive us to question and seek answers on the meaning and purpose of existence."[27] The most crucial thing is not the particular practices we choose but the attitude with which we approach them—the desire to open one's heart to God. This desire is born when we allow ourselves to move from rational thought (mind) to emotive being (heart) that manifests itself in an almost inexplicable yearning for "something more."

> In moments when the clouds of confusion clear and we can see our longing in perspective, it appears as a nagging knowledge that we come from somewhere and exist for some purpose. Our search, then, is a seeking for our deepest roots—not the roots of family, nor of race, nor even of the human species, but our roots as creatures of and in this cosmos.[28]

Spiritual practices bring illumination and focus to the long road between the mind and the heart which is paved with imagination. It is my contention that a primary means of accessing and nurturing the imagination is to engage in some form of creative art.

The Creative Arts as Spiritual Practice

The creative arts are both an avenue through which humans can gain spiritual experience and a means of expressing/shaping/communicating experience of the Divine. One does not need to be a professional artist in order to add creative expression to one's array of spiritual practices. In some cases, art may be the only possible response to the majesty and mystery of God. Furthermore, art offers a form of knowing that cannot be accessed in any other way; it connects us to a source of inner wisdom; it awakens us to awareness.[29] Whenever we are creating, we are also receiving.[30] We are transforming chronos time into kairos time and turning events into memories.[31] "We sometimes forget art's primary role since the dawn of humanity has been to nourish the sacred dimension of life."[32]

Including the creative arts in one's spiritual practice gives one a means of offering a part of oneself to God.[33] When we engage in art for the sheer pleasure of creating, God experiences joy too. "God rejoices in our joy and inspires our creativity."[34] Being in touch with our creativity puts us in touch with our Creator.[35]

During the retreats I conducted with my students, I found that engaging them in creative arts (e.g., painting, collage, mandalas, writing) had the potential to open their minds to the ingenuity, innovation, and imagination that offer pathways to the Divine, whatever their faith tradition happened to be. Support for this idea can be found in the work of Seyyed Hossein Nasr who suggests that all religions have two basic dimensions, the exoteric and the esoteric. "In Judaism and Islam the two dimensions of the tradition as the Talmudic and Kabbalistic or the *Shari'ah* and the *Tariqah* are clearly delineated."[36] Acknowledging that these two dimensions are presently less well-defined in the Christian tradition, Nasr notes that Christianity "did possess at the beginning a distinctly esoteric message which has manifested itself in various ways during the later history of Christianity."[37] Nasr insists that while both dimensions of knowledge are necessary to an integrated, living tradition, most people "live on the periphery of the circle of their own existence, oblivious to the Center which is connected by the esoteric dimension of tradition to the circumference or periphery."[38] A visual representation of this idea is shown below.

Nasr goes on to state that "the esoteric and the mystical have often been castigated as unorthodox."[39] As I have previously noted, at least in twenty-first century American culture the esoteric and mystical are not only unorthodox; they are not valued. Yet I believe experience of them is necessary to our wholeness as

FIGURE 4.1
THE ESOTERIC RADIUS

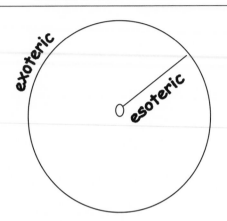

The esoteric is the radius that takes us from the circumference
of our lives to the Ultimate Reality at the center of existence.

Source: Drawn from a verbal description by Seyyed Hossein Nasr, *Knowledge and the Sacred* (New York: State University of New York Press, 1989), 77.

human beings and to the fulfillment of our primary human purpose, relationship with God.

I think engaging in creative arts is one means of gaining access to the esoteric radius that takes us from the circumference of our lives to the Ultimate Reality at the center of existence. Cathy Malchiodi indicates that "art making and the creative source are ways to touch spirit, call it forth, and encounter the sacred."[40] Artist Sara Webb Phillips believes that art, with its "revelatory and sacramental power," is like theology in that both are "concerned with how to make the invisible visible."[41] Thus, I have found the creative arts to be a critical component of retreats offered with the intention of fostering experience of the sacred in college students.

In reflecting on past retreat experiences, students appear to agree:

My most favorite part of the retreat activities was creation of art works. Although I am a non-artistic person who cannot create an elegant piece of artwork, I found a way to express the things that were burdening me most at that time and it relieved me. It opened up the confinement that I was in spiritually.[42]

I think creative arts is a relaxing time to let ourselves express whatever is on our hearts in a totally cool way. Whether it's God's eyes, mandalas, collages, or just coloring, it's a great tool for just letting go and relaxing![43]

We made some type of creative art with every retreat. I still have these items as they remind me of the lessons I learned from those retreats and they help me focus when I need it.[44]

In chapters 5 through 7, I turn at last to a discussion of these retreats. In chapter 8, I offer additional ideas for creative arts and retreat activities. In chapter 9, I review the insights and understandings I gained from the retreats and present my recommendations for offering spiritual retreats for young adults at other institutions.

FIVE

Multifaith Spiritual Retreats for College Students

I n considering the use of multifaith spiritual retreats as a tool in the spiritual and moral formation of college students, three questions are primary: Why is the retreat setting important? Why make the effort to have the retreats be multifaith? Why engage students in the creative arts at such retreats? I believe the answer to the third question has been adequately answered in chapter 4. Let us turn, then, to consideration of the other two questions.

Why Is the Retreat Setting Important?

I believe that the opportunity to experience interfaith community is a critical aspect of the spiritual development of college students in today's global society. Rabbi Howard Addison suggests that "interfaith spiritual experience can lead us to see life as a wheel with the sacred as the living hub and each of us as points along a common rim. As we move down our own spoke toward the core we begin to realize as we come closer to the divine center we, of necessity, become closer to each other."[1]

In my experience, a meaningful, nonthreatening means of affording students an opportunity for interfaith community is to engage them in off-campus spiritual retreats. Dr. David Tacey, at the *Dreaming Landscapes* international campus ministry conference in July 2004, indicated that students need spaces for conversation about spirituality where they do not feel they are being brainwashed. They need spaces in which to address the deep spiritual hunger that is common to all human beings.[2]

In the off-campus setting, students are not distracted by their normal routines and surroundings and can focus on the community that is formed by playing together, praying together, eating together, and creating together with persons whose religions may differ from their own. Luke Timothy Johnson has suggested that obedience to our own faith actually requires "that we maintain an openness to what God is saying in the multiplicity of other voices in the world."[3]

In his book on interfaith spiritual direction, Addison provides a discussion of spiritual types that is useful to our understanding of the importance of the retreat setting. He proposes that we think of a grid with a horizontal axis that runs the gamut from God the Mystery who "defies and transcends all description" to the revealed God, and a vertical axis that runs between the speculative and emotional aspects of human understanding (i.e., between the mind and the heart)[4] (see figure 5.1).

With this grid in mind, Addison then proposes four categories of spirituality. Category one focuses on *speaking about God*. In this category we find the sorts of things common to traditional forms of worship: the study of scripture, the liturgy of the service, and the message or sermon. This category lies in the quadrant between the speculative (mind) and the revealed God.[5]

Category two lies between the revealed God and the emotional apprehension of religious ideas. The primary characteristic of this category is *speaking to God*. Persons who are most comfortable in this category appreciate personal witnessing and rousing music. They will often express a sense of being reborn and tend to exhibit spiritual emotionalism and religious zeal. Persons who consider themselves evangelical tend to fall in this category.[6]

FIGURE 5.1
HOWARD ADDISON'S SPIRITUAL CATEGORIES GRID

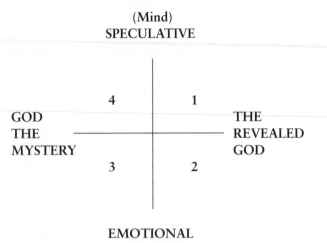

(Mind)
SPECULATIVE

	4	1	
GOD			THE
THE			REVEALED
MYSTERY			GOD
	3	2	

EMOTIONAL
(Heart)

Source: Howard A. Addison, *Show Me Your Way: The Complete Guide to Exploring Interfaith Spiritual Direction* (Woodstock, VT: Skylight Paths Publishing, 2000), 68.

Category three lies in the quadrant between emotional ways of apprehension and God the Mystery. It is in this quadrant that one finds the Christian mystics, the Sufis of Islam, and the Jewish Kabbalists. Persons who are of this spiritual type tend to engage in visualization as a spiritual practice, along with meditation, silent retreats, breath prayer, and chanting. These are the seekers of mystical union. Addison's primary descriptor for this category is *hearing God*.[7]

In category four, we find those who are most at home *serving God*, such as Martin Luther King, Jr. and Mother Theresa. These are people for whom life and work are prayer. These are the social activists, people who engage in ethical and spiritual *mitzvoh*[8] for whom serving others is serving God. This category lies between God the Mystery and the more rational, speculative approach to religion and spirituality.[9] All four categories of spirituality are graphically illustrated in figure 5.2.

FIGURE 5.2

CHARACTERISTICS OF ADDISON'S SPIRITUAL CATEGORIES

(Mind)
SPECULATIVE

4	**1**
Life & work as prayer	Study of scripture
Godly serving of others	Liturgy of worship service
Ethical & spiritual mitzvoh	Sermon
Social activism	
Serving God	*Speaking about God*

GOD THE MYSTERY ——————————— THE REVEALED GOD

(Defies and transcends all description)

(Religious imagery)

3	**2**
Silent retreat	Personal witnessing
Visualization	Rousing music
Meditation	Sense of being reborn
Breath prayer	Spiritual emotionalism
Mystical union	Religious zeal
Chant	Evangelical
Sufism	
Kabbalah	
Hearing God	*Speaking to God*

EMOTIONAL
(Heart)

Source: Adapted from *Show Me Your Way: The Complete Guide to Exploring Interfaith Spiritual Direction* © 2000 by Howard A. Addison (Woodstock, VT: Skylight Paths Publishing, www.skylightpaths.com), 67–71; used by permission. Addison's work is based on Urban T. Holmes's *History of Christian Spirituality* and the "spirituality wheel" developed by Corinne Ware in *Discovering Your Spiritual Type*.

The traditional approach to providing spiritual nurture to college students in our culture has been through corporate worship and Bible studies. These fall into Addison's category one, speaking about God. However, the students with whom I work seem to fall into categories two and four, speaking to God and serving God. This insight is supported by the apparent lack of appeal students find in traditional worship (category one).

Students also express a deep desire to actually hear God in their lives (category three). They are hungry for spiritual practices that will help them to be still and listen for God's voice and put forward other opportunities for firsthand experience of the Divine. The retreat setting offers students a place to encounter God the Mystery in their own experience. Perhaps the best justification for offering spiritual life retreats comes from the experiences of the students themselves:

> As a college student, a lot is going on in your life with peers, academics, and extra curricular activities. It was nice to get away from campus for a weekend and just focus on myself. I tried to forget about the pressure of college as the Spiritual life retreat helped me focus on who I was in relation to God. It was also amazing to hear other people's thoughts and experiences with spirituality.[10]

> What I got from this experience is renewed hope that everything is going to be okay and I'm not in this alone. That all the many things that were bothering me will all turn out okay, or will get done some how. I am a heavily involved person, and just being able to play, be creative, laugh, and cry, lets me relieve some of those pressures in a very positive way.[11]

> This retreat was one of the most spiritually enlightening moments I have experienced in my college career. In the midst of homework, classes, and drama of college friends and acquaintances, I was missing time in my life that I could find "self" within me and just hang out with God. At the retreat, I regained the touch of peace and tranquility.[12]

Why Make the Effort to Have
the Retreats Be Multifaith?

Dr. Ursula King, another speaker at the *Dreaming Landscapes* conference, said students need to engage in conversations that explore the more universal questions that are asked by every religion. She said there is a need for passionate use of our imaginations and a need for community building. She emphasized that we need one another, including each others' faiths coming together in one community of learning.[13] All of these needs can be addressed in an off-campus retreat setting that offers students the opportunity to experience the reality of a God who loves them, whatever their faith tradition.

While the retreat ideas presented in this book can be adapted to include persons of many faith traditions, I must acknowledge that my experience and training lie within Christianity and most of the students with whom I am engaged at the college I serve are Christian. As noted previously, these students tend to fall primarily into category two of Addison's diagram, those whose approach to worship and spirituality involve emotional, zealous, evangelical, born-again personal witnessing with rousing music. I believe my students have turned to this somewhat shallow approach because it is experiential and because their past practice of traditional worship (category one) has left them spiritually hungry. Furthermore, I believe that the retreats I have offered them, which include opportunities to explore the spiritual dimension of creative arts, have provided both experiential spiritual nurture and an opportunity for spiritual growth that can only be achieved through interaction with persons of other faiths or other interpretations of the faith they claim as their own. Sharon Parks has found that "faith develops at the boundary with otherness, when one becomes vulnerable to the consciousness of another, and thus vulnerable to reimagining self, other, world, and 'God.'"[14]

Having determined that retreats offer a viable means of addressing the spiritual needs of college students, let us now consider the nuts and bolts of putting a retreat together. What are the basic resources necessary for a successful retreat? How does one decide where to go, what to do, and how long to stay?

Retreat Basics

Find a facility: It is important to explore camps, retreat centers, and other facilities that might be available at a modest cost in order to get students completely away from campus for the duration of the retreat. One facility my students and I use is owned and operated by a state university and is located forty-five minutes from our campus. This facility offers three stonework cabins with a total of twenty-eight bunk beds, a central lodge with kitchen and fireplace, and an outdoor fire circle for use when weather permits. To take twenty-four to twenty-eight students on a weekend-long retreat at this site costs my program budget about $250. Not all facilities are this inexpensive, but it is extremely helpful to have access to a site that can accommodate a group within the reach of the campus ministry's budget so as to eliminate, or at least reduce, any cost to students themselves.

Certainly it would be possible to have a retreat in a more rugged setting requiring tents and other camping equipment at possibly less cost—but the logistics of acquiring and setting up camping equipment may outweigh the benefits, particularly if the arts activities planned for the retreat are going to require an environment sheltered from the elements. These retreats could also be carried out in an urban setting such as a hotel—but that has the potential to greatly increase the cost per person and loses the direct contact with nature that feeds the spirits of the participants in countless ways. "The theophanic aspect of virgin nature aids in man's [sic] discovery of his [sic] own inner being. Nature is herself a divine revelation with its own metaphysics and mode of prayer."[15]

Feeding the multitude: When it comes to food, one must be sensitive to various dietary requirements. For example, I would not offer bacon or ham at a retreat on which Muslim or Jewish students were participants. Also, one must be sure to offer vegetarian options for students at every meal. I have found it is very wise to ask students when they register if they have any special dietary needs. These days, there is nearly always someone with a lactose intolerance who requires soy milk, for example. A sample menu is available in Appendix A.

Additionally, there is the issue of where one obtains the food. Obviously, items could be divided among the participants with each assigned to bring particular foodstuffs. Here one runs the risk of a student deciding at the last minute not to attend forcing the others to do without the item(s) that student was assigned to bring. Alternatively, the food could be purchased by the retreat planner(s) using the campus ministry's budget or using funds collected as registration fees. At the college I serve, obtaining the food is greatly simplified by the fact that my students are on a meal plan with our campus dining services. I simply have to turn in a menu request and pick up time, along with the students' meal numbers, and then show up at the dining hall to load the food into our vehicles.

Transportation: How will the campus minister and students get to the retreat site? Does the campus ministry have a van (or several) available? When college cars are unavailable, I reserve two or three fifteen-passenger college vans for our retreats. But due to the rollover tendencies of these vehicles highlighted lately in the media, I prefer to take college cars (as many as are available), my personal car, and, if necessary, talk one or more faculty into participating in the retreat and providing a vehicle so we have enough room for transporting people, food, crafts materials, and personal belongings. These retreats are becoming so popular, I may well have to resort to chartering a bus in the near future. Students driving their own vehicles would be a less expensive and less complex solution, but for insurance and liability reasons, this solution is not an option at the college I serve.

Planning the Retreat

When possible, I prefer to involve one or two students in the retreat planning process. This gives them an opportunity to develop some planning and leadership skills, makes my job easier, and gives me a better sense of students' current needs and interests. Furthermore, when students help plan retreats, they usually also help carry them out, again lightening the load on the campus minister/chaplain.

Choosing a theme: The themes for the retreats I have held with my students were chosen to appeal to their desire for spiritual nurture while at the same time not being so specific to one particular faith tradition as to be inhospitable to students from other traditions. These themes include:

- Be Still and Know
- Celebration of Creation
- Finding Wonder in Winter
- God at the Center: Listening to God with Our Lives
- Hectic Pace or Sacred Space
- Into the Woods: A Getaway with God
- Life Is a Spiritual Journey
- Living as God's Beloved: Taken, Blessed, Broken, and Given
- Remembering Our Stories
- The Fabric of Prayer
- Wake Up Moments: Paying Attention to God
- Where Is God at College?

These themes offer students an opportunity to explore who God is, where God is, the reality of God, who they are in relation to God, and other basic questions of human existence. These retreats were built around themes that encouraged students to ask the important questions about their lives and the lives of others.[16] The retreats with themes that do not use what my students call "the G word" (i.e., God), have attracted students who have been alienated by traditional religion or who have never participated in specifically religious practices.

Creating a schedule: A sample retreat schedule for *God at the Center: Listening to God with Our Lives* is presented below. All of the retreats outlined in chapters 6 and 7 follow a similar schedule. However, a word of caution is in order: it is wise not to get too tied to a planned schedule. Sometimes activities or sessions take longer than those who do the planning expect; without flexibility in the schedule, the entire weekend could run amuck. The

Divine Spirit works in her own way and on her own time; we must be open to giving her space to be among us.

Choosing Creative Arts: The creative arts to be included in a retreat should not be chosen randomly. A critical part of the retreat planning process is to think through which activities to include and why. How do the activities relate to the retreat theme? How do they open students' minds and hearts to the Divine? It might be helpful to create an evaluative tool for use in the planning process similar to the *Student Self-Evaluation of Arts Projects* used by Dr. Denise Dombkowski Hopkins at Wesley Theological Seminary in Washington, D.C. A copy of this tool is available in Appendix D. It is critical for the planners of the retreat to mentally walk through every creative arts activity that will be a part of the event so as to list and gather all the necessary crafts supplies.

Sample Retreat Schedule

FRIDAY
4:00 p.m.—Leave Student Center
6:00–6:30—Arrive at Retreat Site
6:30–7:00—Move In & Get Out Food!
7:00–7:45—EAT!
7:45–9:00—"Slowing Down & Making Room for God"
9:00–11:00—Building Community (games, conversation, etc.)

SATURDAY
7:45–8:00 a.m.—"Seeking God in Centering Prayer"
8:30—Breakfast!
9:30–11:00—"Seeking God in Nature"
11:00–12:00—"Seeking God in Silence"
12:15–1:00—Lunch
1:00–2:00—Free Time
2:00–5:00—"Seeking God in Creation"
5:00–6:00—Free Time
6:00–7:00—Dinner
7:00–9:00—"Seeking God in College Life"
9:00–11:00—Sharing Community (games, conversation, etc.)

SUNDAY

7:15–8:00 a.m.—"Seeking God in Guided Meditation"
8:30—Breakfast
9:30–10:30—"Finding God in Reflection"
10:30—Clean-up/Load-up
11:30—Leave for Campus
12:30—Arrive on Campus

Some activities require more advanced planning. For example, I begin gathering magazines for collages in the fall semester for our winter retreat in February. University biology departments are often a good source of nature magazines that offer excellent pictures for creating collages. Since becoming a college chaplain, I see much of my home "junk mail" as an additional retreat resource; advertisements and catalogs I really do not want offer some interesting pictures for my students to use.

As with other costs, it is helpful if the campus ministry has a budget to pay for crafts supplies such that students do not have to pay a fee to attend the retreat. Alternatively, one might engage participants in fund-raisers before the event to help pay for the crafts materials, facility rental, transportation, food, etc.

Publicity and pre-retreat information: I have found it helpful to provide students with a pre-retreat information folder/brochure which includes a list of things students need to be sure to bring (see figure 5.3).

I also always include a paragraph regarding the interfaith inclusive nature of the retreat:

> This spiritual life retreat is for students of all faiths. The program is designed to provide students with an opportunity to experience the gifts of nature, silence, prayer, meditation, creativity, discussion, and fellowship in a retreat setting intended to help us focus on our spiritual development and well-being. Wherever you are on your faith journey, you are invited to join other students in a weekend of spiritual companionship, seeking renewed awareness of God in your life at college.

FIGURE 5.3

Stuff You Need to Bring!

1. Sleeping bag or bedroll
2. Pillow
3. Toothbrush, comb, soap, etc.
4. Towel
5. Tablet or notebook
6. Pen or pencil
7. Holy book from your faith tradition
8. Your imagination
9. An open mind

Optional Stuff

1. Board games (Trivial Pursuit, Backgammon, Risk, etc.)
2. Playing cards
3. Your favorite stuffed animal
4. Flashlight

Preparing a retreat brochure helps the planner(s) advertise the event, provides information to students who are considering whether or not they would like to participate, and serves as a schedule of events during the retreat as well. A complete example of text for a tri-fold retreat brochure is available in the appendices (see Appendix K).

Make a list of responsibilities: Another helpful tool to prepare in advance is a chart of the chores that will need doing during the retreat. Students can sign up for various tasks once the group arrives at the retreat site. By offering this means of volunteering, the retreat leader(s) can be sure everyone does some of the work and that no one gets burdened with doing it all. Examples of chores include making the campfire, cooking various meals, sweeping the lodge, cleaning out the fireplace, sweeping the cabins, cleaning up after meals, etc. A sample chart of chores is provided in Appendix C.

Obviously, I have scattered advice arising from my experience of planning and leading these retreats throughout this book. In chapter 9, I shall summarize my observations and give my recommendations for using these retreats at other institutions.

SIX

Actual Retreat Experiences
Two Examples

I n this chapter I will provide detailed descriptions of two retreats experienced with my students. Both retreats follow a schedule similar to that outlined in chapter 5. As noted elsewhere in this book, if one's time frame is limited to a single day rather than the Friday night through Sunday morning schedule we follow on our retreats, the information presented here can be adapted to accommodate a different time frame.

One possibility would be to use the sessions I have outlined as a series of programs over a period of several weeks, keeping in mind that not all participants will attend every session and the sessions will not be in a retreat setting. Nonetheless, this one session per week approach might prove particularly useful in a congregational setting, especially if the intent is to involve students and other members of the congregation in joint activities.

Another possibility is to adapt the retreat schedule into a single day-long event with two sessions in the morning and two in the afternoon, followed by a brief closing ritual or worship service. If the event were held on a Saturday in a Christian congregational setting, the retreat theme could even be carried over into Sunday worship.

Living as God's Beloved:
Taken, Blessed, Broken, and Given

Ideas for this retreat began with a reading of Henri Nouwen's *Life of the Beloved*.[1] In this book Nouwen, writing to a Jewish friend, describes all of humanity as being taken, blessed, broken, and given by God. The scripture which is basic to Nouwen's discussion is Matthew 3:13–17, the Baptism of the Lord, in which Jesus hears the voice of God saying, "This is my son, the Beloved, with whom I am well pleased" (Mt. 3:17 [NRSV]). Nouwen writes to his friend:

> For many years I had read these words and even reflected upon them in sermons and lectures, but it is only since our talks in New York that they have taken on a meaning far beyond the boundaries of my own tradition. Our many conversations led me to the inner conviction that the words, "You are my Beloved" revealed the most intimate truth about all human beings, whether they belong to any particular tradition or not.
>
> Fred, all I want to say to you is "You are the Beloved," and all I hope is that you can hear these words as spoken to you with all the tenderness and force that love can hold. My only desire is to make these words reverberate in every corner of your being—"You are the Beloved."
>
> The greatest gift my friendship can give to you is the gift of your Belovedness. I can give that gift only insofar as I have claimed it for myself. Isn't that what friendship is all about: giving to each other the gift of our Belovedness?[2]

For college students searching for meaning, searching for relationship, searching for answers to the big questions that lead to worthy dreams, what could be more wonderful than to truly understand that they are God's Beloved? Exposing students to this idea and helping them to receive the gift of their Belovedness was the focus of this retreat. I broke it down into the following sessions: Friday night, "Taken;" Saturday morning, "Blessed;" Saturday afternoon, "Broken;" Saturday night, "Given;" and Sunday morning, a service of worship in which we reflected on what each of us learned, discovered, or otherwise found particularly meaningful during the retreat.

Because this retreat was scheduled just a month into the spring semester, student involvement in the planning process came only after the theme and basic outline had been set. Students, when they returned to campus after their winter break, helped decide which activities should be included to help participants experience their Belovedness. It was in our planning discussion that we decided to include Isaiah 43:1–7 in addition to Matthew 3:13–17 because my students share my desire to make these retreats meaningful to students of all faiths. The text from Isaiah surely conveys the message of our Belovedness when God says, "You are precious and honored in my sight . . . and I love you" (Isaiah 43:4).

When the retreat weekend arrived, the participants gathered at the student center parking area late Friday afternoon to load personal belongings and food into college vehicles (one van and three cars). There were fourteen participants: twelve students, one faculty member, and myself. Once we had loaded the vehicles, we gathered in a room in the student center for instructions on where to go when we arrived. I also made sure each driver had a map to the retreat site and my cell phone number. Then I offered a prayer that we might have a safe journey and truly become a community as we sought closer relationship with the Divine and with each other.

Upon arrival at the retreat site, we unloaded our food and personal belongings, got settled in the cabins, put the food away, and made dinner. After cleaning up from dinner, we set up a circle of chairs in the main room of the lodge and gathered for our first session.

Friday Night—"Taken":

Materials: Bibles in different translations
Paper (for those who neglected to bring a
tablet or notebook)
Pens or pencils
Flip Chart
Markers

To begin this session, I again welcomed everyone and asked each person to introduce himself/herself by telling us their name, their major, their class level, and why they decided to come on this retreat. Answers varied and included, "So-and-So invited me," "To get away from campus," "To have fun," "To work on my prayer life," and "I've been on other retreats and could hardly wait for this one!"

Following these introductions, I asked the students to think for a moment about ways that our time together could be really meaningful, things we could do to help one another be a part of the community we were forming, and how to make this a "safe space" in which to share some of our deeper feelings. Their thoughts included really listening to one another, making an agreement that what was expressed and shared on the retreat needed to be kept confidential, and being sure that everyone's voice was valued.

Next I reminded them of the theme for the retreat and the topics for each session (which all of them were familiar with because they each got a brochure when they registered). I explained how these had grown out of reading Nouwen's book in which he, as a Christian priest, had been writing to a Jewish friend. I also pointed out, for any students to whom this might not be familiar, that the verbs *taken*, *blessed*, *broken*, and *given* remind those of us who are Christian about what Jesus did with the bread during his final meal with his disciples the night before his crucifixion.

Next I introduced the idea of "speed bumps" in biblical interpretation, "details that catch your attention and demand closer inspection because they have evoked particularly strong feelings, or because they seem unclear, especially vivid, out of place, or inconsistent."[3] Noting that we would be listening for "speed bumps," I then asked one of the students to read the text from Matthew while the rest of us followed along. Some students had brought their own Bibles. For those who did not or who do not own a Bible, I had brought a supply including the NRSV, NIV, KJV, and *The Message*,[4] the latter being the version which most appeals to my current students.

One major "speed bump" came in v. 14, "John would have prevented him . . ." (NRSV) or "John tried to deter him . . . " (NIV). This seemed pretty "gutsy" to my students even for Jesus' cousin. We talked about having the audacity to say "I don't think so" to a person John was ready to proclaim as the Messiah. Eventually we concluded this indicated a very down-to-earth relationship between Jesus and John, just the sort of relationship the students might have with a cousin of their own. This idea gave my students great delight.

Next I suggested that we look back at v. 11 where John describes Jesus as one "whose sandals I am not fit to carry" (NIV). I asked them if possibly John might have been suffering from low self-esteem. One of the reasons I raised this question is because I know some of my students have problems with self-esteem. They were surprised by my suggestion about John but as our discussion continued, it appeared to have offered an opening for them to really get into the story and identify with its characters. Eventually we concluded that telling God "I'm not good enough to do what you ask of me" is rather arrogant. If God thinks one is good enough, one would be pretty audacious to disagree!

Another focus of our discussion centered on the Holy Spirit descending like a dove. This brought us to consider what else we knew of the Holy Spirit in the Bible. One student brought up the beginning of Genesis where the Spirit moves across the face of the water. Another brought up the tongues of fire at Pentecost in the Book of Acts. The water and fire would eventually help us connect this text to Isaiah 43:1–7.

Finally, our discussion of the Matthean text centered on the voice of God saying, "This is my son, the Beloved, with whom I am well pleased" (Mt. 3:17 [NRSV]). I asked the students to close their eyes for a few moments and try to imagine themselves being baptized by John in the Jordan River. I asked them to imagine what they felt, what they saw, what they tasted, what they smelled, and what they heard. Imagining hearing the voice of God telling them they were God's Beloved with whom God was well pleased was a very moving experience for them.

We then moved on to a discussion of the passage from Isaiah in which our "speed bumps" included the end of v. 1: "I have called you by name" and, in v. 2, the images of waters (lakes?) and rivers that are juxtaposed with fire that will not burn; flame that will not consume. We noted in our discussion that fire and water cannot coexist. They are two extremes of nature—and in this verse, God promises to be with us through encounters with both. To the ancient Hebrews, surely these images again recalled the Exodus when Moses drew *water* from a rock and they followed God's presence as a pillar of *fire* through the wilderness. Flame that does not consume, also caused us to think of Exodus 3 in which Moses encounters the bush that is burning but not consumed. Remembering this story caused us to reflect on the outdoors which we would explore on Saturday—holy ground.

Finally, I suggested that we try to outline the passage to see what ideas might be repeated. This is what we came up with:

A   created/formed
B   Do not fear.
C   I have redeemed you.
D   I have called you by name; you are mine.
E   I will be with you.
C' I ransomed you.
      V. 4   SINCE YOU ARE PRECIOUS AND HONORED
             IN MY SIGHT AND BECAUSE I LOVE YOU
C" I will give people and nations in return for you.
B' Do not fear.
E' I am with you.
D' Everyone who is called by my name.
A' created/formed

Outlining the passage in this way proved to be quite helpful. We then saw that it began and ended with God's creation; twice we are told not to fear because God is with us, has called us by name, and has redeemed us (in fact, this part "C" occurs three times). Perhaps the most significant result of this outline was the emphasis it placed on v. 4, taking us right back to Matthew 3:13–17—the idea of being God's Beloved. They truly began to see themselves as "taken" by God.

The students really enjoyed this way of doing Bible study. I strongly recommend this "roadmap" method outlined in Appendix F, even if one never gets beyond the suggestion to pay attention to "speed bumps." Even in other groups on campus, now and then I will hear a student who participated in this retreat say,

"Wait a minute! I just had a speed bump!" He or she may have to explain the term to the others, but it has become a part of the way these students have learned to engage one another in dialogue.

Once we concluded our Bible study, we turned to the creative arts activity chosen for the evening to reinforce the ideas that had come out of our discussion: Acrostic Poetry Writing. The instructions for this activity, including an example based on the word *Beloved*, are included in chapter 8. Following the writing and sharing of our poems, students spent the rest of the evening (and into the wee hours of the morning) playing board games, playing cards, sitting by the fire, engaging one another in conversation, roasting marshmallows, etc.

Saturday Morning—"Blessed":

> Materials: Scissors (at least one pair for every two people)
> Glue sticks (at least one stick for every two people)
> Poster board (11" x 14")—at least one per person
> Magazines—a good variety; at least three per person—all will be shared by the entire group, but having a sufficient supply per person to begin with avoids stifling creativity.
> Sufficient copies of the texts from Isaiah and Matthew for each person to have easy access

For this session the group gathered around the large rectangle of tables we had set up for breakfast. A piece of paper with the texts from Isaiah and Matthew was distributed to each place at the table. The night before, I had asked a student if he would be willing to begin our session with a prayer of blessing, to which his response was affirmative. Following his prayer, I reminded the group of our discussion the previous evening and asked if any of them had further reflections on either scripture.

They were still amazed by all they had discovered in the two texts and were feeling awed by how much God really loved them. That led naturally into a brief discussion of what it means to be blessed by God. Much of this was expressed in terms of specific blessings such as family, food, shelter, this place to have a retreat, friends, talents, intelligence, nature, etc. But I also introduced the idea of stewardship—that part of receiving a blessing is caring for it and using it. We eventually arrived at an understanding that using the gifts God gives us can be a blessing to others.

We then moved into the collage making process (see chapter 8). I suggested that students might find it helpful to read back over the two texts we'd been discussing to see if there might be a question they could respond to through the process of making a collage. One possibility might be "How has God blessed me?" I told them they could certainly use that question but that they should first look for other possibilities that might arise for them out of the two texts. The question that emerged for me as I engaged in this process with my students was "What does it mean to be made and formed by God?"

There are many reasons for retreat leaders to engage in all the creative arts activities planned for the participants. One is to be able to judge the amount of time others need to complete their projects. Perhaps the most important reason is in order to experience the entire retreat with the students rather than setting oneself apart. Also, self-care is a crucial aspect of campus ministry (or any other form of ministry); participating in these activities with the students is a way to nurture one's own soul.

Saturday Afternoon—"Broken":

Materials: Scissors (at least one pair for every two people)
Poster board—any size—for making cut out shapes
Muslin—One piece 18" x 72" per person
Tumble-Dye spray dye[5]
Bucket or pan of water
Paper
Pens

After lunch we gathered for our afternoon session in a circle of chairs—the same room arrangement we had used the evening before. I introduced the topic of "brokenness" by acknowledging that experiences of brokenness are difficult to talk about, especially in our culture that has a practice of avoiding public tears, rarely ever talks about death and dying, and communicates a general message that everyone should be able to pull themselves out of any trouble without much help (or no help at all). Consequently, troubles are rarely discussed beyond small, intimate groups. I reminded them that we had agreed on Friday night that we would make our retreat space a safe place for us to express some of these difficult things.

Next I told the group that this afternoon we were going to take a closer look at one of the Psalms. I let them know there are several different kinds of psalms and acknowledged that they were probably most familiar with psalms of praise. I pointed out that the psalms, however, express a wide range of human emotions some of which actually take God to task for God's apparent absence or seeming failure to act on behalf of the petitioner or the community. I told the students that these are called psalms of lament—and for whatever reason, they have been little used or even ignored by many church communities. "Something is . . . wrong if praise of God finds a place in Christian worship while lament does not" for we cannot hope to have a whole and honest relationship with God if we do not allow ourselves to express half the range of human feeling.[6] The laments, more so even than the psalms of praise, are "insistent upon relationship with God as crucial for our lives."[7]

I asked my students how many of them had ever cried out, "I don't know *how* to pray!" I knew a number of them would raise their hands. I believe many factors lie behind this lament including their image of God, their belief that doubt undermines faith, their understanding of prayer as something formal best left to those trained in theology, and the probability that they've been exposed to very few models of prayer.

I suggested to them that the Psalms can be a book of lessons on how to pray. I then asked about types of prayers one might offer. Petitions for help topped their list, followed by thanksgiving (usually for help received) and prayers of confession. Some of them expressed the thought that prayer is useless because "God never listens anyway." They were aghast when I asked if they had ever said that to God. It doesn't occur to them to complain to God because no one has ever modeled such prayer to them, much less suggested that it might be okay. "Many Christians think that 'complaining in faith' is a contradiction in terms; if one complains, one is not faithful."[8]

I told them that this afternoon we were going to focus on a psalm of lament as a means of exploring the idea of human brokenness and to help them broaden their understanding of prayer. My intent was to help them create some of the stability that has been missing because God for too long has seemed distant, unreal, uncaring, and judgmental.

Turning to a consideration of Psalm 13, we read it through together in our various translations, watching for "speed bumps." The first one noted was that verses 1 through 4 are positively railing at God. Then, suddenly, in verses 5 and 6 the psalmist returns to praise for God and rejoicing in the bounty God has given. I told the students that this is a common structure of psalms of lament; usually they conclude with a confession of trust and/or a vow of praise.[9]

Another "speed bump" was the force of the demand for an answer from God in verse three, "Consider and answer me, O Lord my God!" (NRSV). This led to a discussion of the various emotions expressed by the psalmist—anger, fear, sorrow, abandonment, frustration, and, at the end, thanksgiving and joy. By looking at the psalm so closely, students really began to identify with the psalmist, comparing his feelings to those they have experienced themselves. We concluded with the new understanding that over the course of human history laments have been a natural response to brokenness. I then reminded everyone of the two theme scriptures for our retreat that suggest that God is present with us in times of trouble, threat, and danger as well as times of life-changing blessing.

After our discussion, we broke into small groups, two groups of three and two groups of four. In these groups we shared with one another what comes to mind when we think of brokenness— and when or if we had experienced God in a circumstance of brokenness. We also gave thought to times when we have caused someone else to experience brokenness. One person in each small group was asked to be responsible for keeping track of their ideas so they could report back to the larger group.

In keeping with the concept that the deeper things of this retreat need to remain confidential, I have chosen not to include the results of this discussion beyond saying that few of us seem to reach college age without experiences of brokenness, some of them absolutely profound. Once we had shared with each other what came out of our small groups, we turned to creative responses to all of the scriptures we had discussed so far on our retreat. I encouraged everyone to take part of the afternoon to try writing a lament or at least to reflect on the idea of brokenness. (Note: It is very important after any retreat session packed with emotion that the retreat leader be available to any participants who need help processing the feelings that were evoked by the session.)

Our other creative activity for the afternoon was to begin our prayer shawls. I introduced the concept of prayer shawls, both as ritual objects used in various faith traditions (e.g., Christianity, Judaism, and Buddhism) and as a means through which students might express their reactions to the scriptures we had discussed. I also suggested that they might find it helpful to think of their shawl as a "cloak of protection," something that they might don when they are feeling the need to find sacred space in the tumult of college life; a place to set themselves apart, sort of a "tent" to enclose themselves with God; a space in which they might find solace and/or healing for brokenness; a safe space in which to confess before God whatever might need confessing and to seek God's forgiveness.

Then I explained the basic procedure of wetting the muslin and wringing it out and then applying the dye from the spray bottles. Before the retreat I had made several examples of how the dye might be used, including the ways in which it "bleeds" or does not, depending on how moist the muslin is when the dye is sprayed on the cloth. I also showed them an example of using a leaf to create silhouetted shapes in the design and talked about the effects they could achieve by bunching or folding the cloth. Additionally, I suggested that they might want to cut shapes out of poster board to make silhouettes. Some students were ready immediately to go outside and begin applying the dye; others began by creating cutout shapes or looking for leaves or other natural objects to use in the dyeing process.

The actual application of the dyes was fairly quick. When students finished and had hung their shawls on bushes or in trees to dry, they were free to sit by the fire, go outside, or go to their cabins to work on their written reflections. Once they had taken time to reflect, students had the rest of the afternoon to play games, hike, nap, study, add to their collages, or whatever.

It was about ten minutes after the first shawl was hung up to dry that we hit our first snag. This was winter. The shawls could not dry outside—they just froze into colorful stiff boards. Fortunately I had brought a lot of plastic with which to cover the tables when we painted the shawls (which we could not do until they were dry). I also had some clothesline ropes I had used to tie my bedroll together. We strung the ropes across one end of the big lodge room with plastic sheets spread beneath them and laid the now stiff shawls across the ropes. They soon began to droop and drip as the drying process began. (Note: a concise, step-by-step description of the prayer shawl making process is included in chapter 8).

Saturday Night—"Given":

Materials: Flip Chart
Markers
Fabric paint
Paper towels
Paint brushes (optional)
Tables (we used 8-foot folding tables on which three students could work at a time, two on each side and one on the end; the end person did not have the entire shawl on the table at any one time, but the paint quickly dries to a consistency that does not run)
Plastic drop cloths to cover tables
Scissors
Macramé cord
Thread & sewing needles

For this evening session, we again gathered in our circle of chairs. After dinner, we had moved the tables toward the back of the room, removed the plastic drop cloths from beneath the now dry dyed shawls, spread the plastic across the tables and taped it down. Once we gathered in our circle, I again called the students' attention to the four verbs that were the focus of this retreat. I told them that tonight we would concentrate on *given*. I asked everyone to think about what gifts they had to give. What special blessings were theirs that might be shared? What talents did they have? In what ways did they feel called to give of themselves and/or to serve others? How did these ideas relate to the texts from Isaiah and Matthew? Discussion seemed a little slow, so I asked them to break into small groups again to consider these things. After about fifteen minutes we regathered in our large circle to hear what was discovered in each small group.

As we heard the group reports about their various gifts, we made a list on the flip chart. These students are very service oriented and they began to see connections between their special talents and ways these might be shared with others. They even suggested that the creative arts they had been producing during the retreat are gifts that could be passed on, whether that meant reading a poem or lament they had written, giving away their creations as gifts, teaching someone else to do these activities, etc.

After our discussion, each participant found a place at one of the tables and I showed them some different techniques for applying paint to their prayer shawls such as simple application from the bottle, spreading the paint with a paper towel or their fingers, outlining an image in the dye, etc. I encouraged them to really *look* at their shawls before they began applying paint to see what designs had appeared during the dyeing process that they might want to highlight with paint. I also asked them to think yet again about the texts from Isaiah and Matthew, as well as their experiences during the weekend, as they considered what to put on their shawls.

As students begin to finish their painting, we gathered around the fire and sang a few songs. Then, several students asked if we could read our acrostic poems, display our collages, and/or read our laments as participants felt moved to share with the group. At the end of the campfire, I encouraged everyone to consider overnight what word they might use to sum up their experience of the weekend or one meaningful word they would take with them as they went home. I told them these words would be shared during our worship service on Sunday morning.

Then, before we broke into our community/game/conversation time, I passed out retreat evaluation forms with a plea that they be filled out and returned sometime before we left the next day. I also showed them how to attach macramé cord ties to the corners of their shawls, an activity they could engage in while the paint was still drying (as long as they left the shawls resting on the tables) or after they returned to campus on Sunday.

Sunday Morning—Reflections:

Following breakfast, our Sunday morning service was a time of reflection on "Living as God's Beloved: Taken, Blessed, Broken, and Given." It included yet another reading of the scriptures from Isaiah and Matthew, sharing of the word each of us had thought of during the night, singing, and a prayer circle during which a candle was passed from person to person. Each participant held the candle as long as they wished and prayed silently or shared their prayer with the group. Finally we sang David Haas's song *"You Are Mine,"*[10] and I gave each participant a dove tac-pin[11] to remind them of their Belovedness. Then I reminded them about their evaluation forms (many of which had already been turned in) and we cleaned the camp, loaded the vehicles, and returned to campus.

Celebration of Creation

I planned this retreat with one of our senior Religious Studies majors who is interested in devoting her life to retreat ministries. Knowing that the woods would be resplendent with the colors of Autumn in mid-October, we decided to celebrate creation and our Creator. In preparation for the retreat, the student searched the Internet for references to nature in the sacred texts of various world religions. I also supplied a number of resource books including Matthew Fox's *One River, Many Wells: Wisdom Springing from Global Faiths.*[12] A complete list of the resource books I provided is available in Appendix G.

The arrangements for food, transportation, etc., were much like our other retreats. We had twenty-one participants. We left the college's student center in a frog-strangling downpour that began just after we got the vehicles loaded and which lasted about half the distance to the retreat site. We were all relieved when the rain stopped such that we did not have to get soaked while unloading once we had arrived.

Friday Night—"Big Rocks" and "Snowballs in October":

Materials: A glass jar
              A rock almost too big to fit into the jar—but
                 which does go in the jar
              Smaller rocks
              Sand
              A glass of water
              Plain white paper
              Markers or pens

Following our arrival, move-in, dinner, and clean-up, we moved chairs into a semicircle facing the fire we had built in the fireplace at one end of the lodge. I introduced the theme for the retreat, "Celebration of Creation," and led the group in a brief discussion of the need for our time together to be "safe space" in which to share deep feelings and personal spiritual insights. Then I suggested, because we had a number of people who were attending a college spiritual life retreat for the first time, that we go around the circle to introduce ourselves and tell each other what we hoped to get out of the experience. Of the twenty students, twelve were first-time participants.

Next I noted that the session listed on the schedule for the evening was "Snowballs in October," but before we explored what that meant I wanted us to talk about big rocks. Naturally enough, they looked a bit puzzled as I brought out a jar and placed a rock inside that nearly filled it. As I proceeded to put in smaller rocks, sand, and finally water, asking them after each addition if the jar was now full, they were entertained, but still wondering why I was doing these things. When we had all agreed that there was absolutely no more room in the jar, I asked them what would have happened if I had put things in the jar in the opposite order, beginning with water. They decided the sand would have made a lot of water spill out, that I might have been able to force in a few of the smaller rocks, and that the big rock would never go in at all. Then I suggested that they needed to think of the most important things in their lives as their big rocks." If they did not put them in the "jars" of their day-to-day living first, they would come to the end of each day with no more room for their "big rocks."[13]

This activity led us to a consideration of God as one of the biggest "rocks" and following the discussion that ensued, I distributed pieces of plain white paper and colored markers. Then I asked them to think about their images of God, write them on the paper, and when they were through, to wad the paper up into a "snowball" and throw it across the circle, being careful not to throw their contributions into the fire. I explained that when everyone was finished writing and throwing "snowballs," we would each unwad and read whatever paper was within reach, thus making each person's thoughts more or less anonymous (see further discussion of the "snowball" activity in chapter 8).

In planning this endeavor, I had lost sight of the enthusiasm that emerges in students when they are given permission to throw things indoors. The "snowball" fight that evening was quite vigorous and included lots of laughter as paper balls went flying around the room.

Finally we settled down to read the writings to one another; like snowflakes, no two were identical. This naturally led to a discussion of God being bigger than any images we are capable of constructing. We also had a conversation about diversity in nature, in God, and in human responses to God—including a variety of religions around the world.

Next we sang a number of songs, including *In the Bulb there Is a Flower, Come and Find the Quiet Center,* and *How Great Thou Art.* To end our time around the fire, I brought out marshmallows, Hershey bars, and graham crackers. The students, of course, knew exactly what to do with these ingredients. For the rest of the evening we played various board games and card games, engaged in conversation, sat by the fire, etc.

Saturday Morning—"Prayer Rocks" and "Images of God":

Materials: Flat rocks from a garden shop or other source
                      (dark-colored or black are best)
                  Marker pens that write in white, gold, or silver
                  Poster board at least 11" x 14"—bring enough
                      for each student to have *at least* two pieces
                  Chalks and/or craypas and/or colored markers
                  Newspaper
                  Black Ink (preferably water-soluble)
                  Cotton string or yarn cut in 18-inch lengths

Following breakfast, we left the room arranged in the large rectangle of tables around which we had gathered to eat and covered the tables in newspaper, taped down with masking tape. I brought out a bowl of flat black rocks and two silver markers and explained the concept of prayer rocks (see chapter 8). I told them the rocks and markers would be available on a table in one corner of the room throughout the rest of the retreat for them to come write prayers whenever they wished. Then we had five minutes of silent prayer, which we closed by singing *Sanctuary.*

Next we distributed string, bowls of ink (one for every two people), boxes of oil crayons (craypas), colored markers, and two pieces of poster board per person. Then I asked them to think about their "snowballs" from the night before and told them that our current activity was intended to help them tap into their imaginations by creating spontaneous images with string soaked in ink[14] (see chapter 8: "Ink and Craypas Drawings").

Unlike many of the creative arts activities I use with students on retreats, I had not tried this one previously. As we got into the process, we found that it was helpful to let the strings sit in the bowls for a minute or so to really absorb the ink. As our creations dried, I encouraged students to begin looking at their drawings to see what images of nature or other meaningful shapes might be hidden in them. "Oh, look!" "Wow!" and "It's a whale!" were some of the surprised comments that began to fill the room. When the ink was dry we used craypas and markers to highlight, outline, or otherwise enhance our drawings. The students really seemed to be enjoying this activity. Unfortunately, I was to miss the next two hours of the retreat. I had noticed that one of the students was not participating and went to the cabins to check on her. She was feeling really quite ill and asked if I could take her back to campus. This was the first time such a situation had arisen and I was glad we were only 40 miles from the college (as opposed to the church camp we had used the first couple of years which was 150 miles distant). I agreed to take her back and went to make arrangements with some of the senior students to carry on with lunch in my absence.

Apparently after I left and before they began to prepare lunch, the students shared their drawings with one another and discussed the images they found in them. I was sorry to have missed this sharing, but am delighted that they were so engaged by the activity that they wanted to disclose their insights to one another. They had also used masking tape to put their pictures on the walls all around the lodge.

I got back to the retreat site about 1:00 p.m., just as the students were finishing their postlunch cleanup. The schedule had free time for them until 3:00. Several students asked if we had enough materials for them to make more drawings during this time, so I set aside twenty pieces of poster board we would need Saturday evening and told them to go ahead with what was left. I was really quite impressed that they had found this activity so meaningful and enjoyable that they wanted more of it.

Saturday Afternoon—"Nature Walk and Collection"

There are a number of trails through woods and meadows at the site we now use for our retreats. Early Saturday morning I had checked out one of them that had ended in a maze in a cornfield. (One of the students who discovered the same spot during his free time Saturday afternoon dubbed it the maize maze.)

At 3:00 p.m. we gathered for our nature walk. I told students that this would be a different sort of walk because we were not going to talk to one another. Rather, walking in silence, with pauses now and then, I wanted them to look at and listen intently to their surroundings. I spoke briefly about the Buddhist concept of mindfulness—paying attention to the moment and being present through letting go of intentional thoughts. I told them this would be a "zen walk" of ten to fifteen minutes at what might be a slower pace than they would normally go along a trail. Silently, in single file, we set forth, our ears filled with the sounds of forty feet shuffling through autumn leaves on the forest floor.

At the last minute, as we approached the beginning of the trail I had walked that morning, knowing at least one student had already been down that path too, I turned and started down another path. In some ways this was a really foolish decision—taking nineteen students down a path I'd not walked myself in over a year. What was to have been a walk of ten to fifteen minutes turned into forty because this path was longer than I had remembered and included two places in which we had to negotiate creek crossings via slippery mud banks, rocks, and downed trees because two of the four bridges were "out." But despite these surprises and difficulties, the "zen walk" turned out to be the most meaningful part of the retreat for several students. Several times along our way we just stopped to listen and clear our ears of the sound of crunching leaves.

When we emerged from the woods near the cabins, I led the group over to the outdoor campfire circle where we sat to talk about what we had seen, heard, and otherwise experienced. One student noted the different colors of light coming through the autumn leaves; another spoke of bird songs. A number of them mentioned how loud we were as a group crunching leaves beneath our feet. Several spoke of their difficulty at first in not talking yet how "cool" it was when we stopped and were totally silent in the midst of the woods listening to the sounds of nature. Following this discussion, I turned them loose to go collect objects from nature which they would use that evening in a project involving gluing their prizes to poster board. It was important to mention this detail so they would come back with items that could be glued down. Then it was time for the cooks, including me, to go begin preparing dinner.[15]

Saturday Night—*"Celebrating Creation through Holy Texts"*

Materials: 11" x 14" poster board—at least one piece per
                   participant
               Liquid white glue
               Colored markers
               Craypas
               Puffy paints in a variety of colors
               Natural materials collected by participants
                   earlier in the day

After dinner I had a couple of students help me set up for our evening session. We got out the many books I had brought (see Appendix G) as well as several copies of the texts from World Scriptures pulled off the Internet by the student who had helped me plan the retreat, and placed them on a table at one side of the room. We also put several different translations of the Bible on the book table. We distributed poster board, glue, markers, craypas, and puffy paint around the other tables still set up in a large rectangle from dinner. As students began to gather, I asked them to be sure they had brought the nature items they had collected during the afternoon.

I began this session by referring back to the diversity of ideas about God which had been expressed in our "snowball" activity the evening before and the diversity of images that had emerged from our ink and craypas drawings on Saturday morning. I then pointed to the display of books and told them for this activity they were invited to look through these resources to find a quotation that was especially meaningful to them. They would then write this on the poster board (using markers, craypas, paint, or anything else that seemed right to them). Once their quotation was in place, they would then glue their natural treasures onto the board to frame or otherwise enhance the text.

While we had originally planned to have the sharing of these quotations be a part of our Sunday morning celebration, it became obvious as folks were finishing their creations that many of them did not want to wait; they wanted to share and see what others had done right away. So I went with the flow, once more following my intuition on this retreat rather than stifling this interaction just so we could "stick to the schedule." The quotations were as beautiful and varied as the students' reasons for choosing them.

At the end of this session, we reviewed our options for the morning—what time they wanted to have breakfast in order to leave before another group arrived, how much time they would need for cleaning up the retreat site, etc. Then I handed out evaluation forms and asked that they take some time to fill them out before we left the next day.

With everyone helping, cleaning up from our final Saturday session was swift. While we were so engaged, a couple of the students went to the outdoor fire circle to light the fire they had laid earlier in the day. By the time the rest of us got outside, the flames were soaring and spreading their warmth to the edges of the ring where the benches were. It was a crisp evening, perfect for an outdoor campfire (and much drier than the evening before). We sang songs and then talked on into the night, sharing stories of family and faith, weaving their strands together in a tapestry of revelation as our knowledge of one another deepened at this outdoor hearth.

Sunday Morning—"Celebrating God's Creation"

Though we had all stayed up late the night before, the group was very responsible about getting moving on Sunday morning, knowing we had to be cleaned up and gone by 10:00 a.m. because another group was due at 11:00 a.m. Most of the students had completed their evaluations and left them in a stack in the lodge sometime during the night after the campfire. At breakfast I made a plea that the rest of these forms be turned in before we left.

Following breakfast, we mutually decided to clean the lodge and cabins and stow all our gear in the vehicles before our closing session so that the session could be our final experience together on this retreat. Though it was very chilly (we had to scrape frost off the car windshields before moving them from the parking lot to the loading area near the cabins), we decided to have our "Celebration of Creation" outdoors.

On Saturday afternoon during our free time, I had dismantled the contents of the jar used to demonstrate "Big Rocks" on Friday night. Now, as we packed to leave, I left out a box that included the jar, the big rock, and the little rocks, as well as the prayer rocks that had been created throughout the previous day and evening. Once everything else was in our cars and the camp was clean, we gathered at the outdoor fire circle.

As the students arrived, I handed each of them one of the decorated prayer rocks—then went around the circle giving out more rocks until some students had three each, an obvious indicator that this activity had been another with which the students really connected. After distributing the rocks, I invited everyone to sit in silence for a few minutes and just listen to the chorus of Creation all around us. Then, in a gentle voice, I asked them to read the words and/or describe the images written/drawn on the prayer rocks they held. I ended this sharing time by asking God to hear these and all the other prayers that had welled up in us during our retreat, whether expressed or still held within our hearts.

Next we sang *I Will Call upon the Lord*, which includes the line, ". . . and blessed be the Rock." This led quite naturally to remembering our "big rocks" demonstration from Friday night. I held up the jar with the big rock in it and once more emphasized the importance of putting the big rocks in our lives first. Then I gave each of them one of the smaller rocks we had used on Friday evening, to take home as a reminder to make time and space for the big rocks. Finally I told them I hoped the peace, insights, and new beginnings from this retreat would continue to bless them in the months and years ahead. Then I invited them to put all the prayer rocks on one of the benches at the fire circle so they could retrieve the rocks they had decorated if they wished to take them. We said our good-byes with many hugs, gathered our prayer rocks, got in the vehicles, and drove back to the campus.

Conclusion

It is my hope that these two detailed reports of my retreat experiences with my students have sparked the reader's imagination and provided sufficient information for you to plan and lead retreats of your own. Every experience with every group will be unique; there is no single "right" way to conduct retreats. As long as you plan something meaningful, invite people to participate, and leave plenty of room for the Holy Spirit to inspire and surprise, you should find participants—and yourself—looking forward to the next one.

For additional encouragement and inspiration, outlines for seven other retreats I have conducted with my students are included in chapter 7. In chapter 8, I offer detailed descriptions of numerous creative arts endeavors and other activities I have used to enhance students' retreat experiences. These are resources that can be adapted to numerous Christian Education events and formats within local congregations and are not limited to use with young adults.

SEVEN

Additional Retreat Outlines

God at the Center: Listening to God with Our Lives

This retreat helps participants discover ways God acts in their lives and helps them focus on putting God at the center. Sessions can be designed around subthemes that are appropriate to your particular group. The retreat is based on the creation of paper flowers, the petals of which symbolize the various ways in which God draws us into relationship with the Divine. In order to have enough petals to make a flower, I recommend that retreat planners choose at least three subthemes.

Art supplies: Construction paper, crayons, scissors, glue, and materials for any other activities chosen from chapter 8 or other resources.

Subthemes: Invitation, Grace, Blessing, Refuge, Guidance, Understanding, Love, etc.

Over the course of this retreat, students will decorate flower petals with words and symbols that depict for them the theme of each session. I would make Petal #1 "Invitation" and discuss with students ways in which God invites us into relationship and ways in which we invite God to be a part of our lives. Petal #2 might be "Refuge," a theme that resonates with students as they retreat from campus life and as darkness settles on the first night of their retreat together. Petal #3 might be "Blessing" as a way to focus on the gifts of a new day. Petal #4 might be "Guidance," particularly if the retreat is held in a setting that lends itself to walks in the woods. Discussion could include some of the Psalms that ask God to show us the way, such as Psalm 25:4–5:

> [4]Show me Your ways, O LORD;
> Teach me Your paths.
> [5]Lead me in Your truth and teach me,
> For You are the God of my salvation;
> On You I wait all the day.

Once the number of sessions has been decided and a subtheme chosen for each, the retreat facilitator is ready to consider other activities that might be useful in exploring these themes, such as

FIGURE 7.1
**PETAL PATTERN AND CENTER CIRCLE
FOR "GOD AT THE CENTER"**

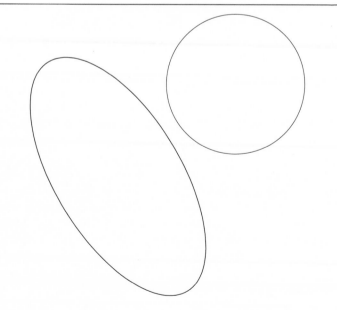

making collages, mandalas, prayer shawls, God's eyes, acrostic poetry writing, journaling, centering prayer, guided meditation, taking a hike, etc.

The final session of this retreat is "God at the Center"—during which students decorate the center circle of the flower and glue the whole thing together. Discussion might focus on ways participants can make God more central in their lives as college students, whatever their faith tradition might be.

When putting the flowers together, it is helpful for students to have two center circles, one to glue the petal ends down upon and the other to decorate and overlay as the centerpiece of the flower. Petals may be cut using the pattern provided on the previous page (figure 7.1) or freehand—as long as they are large enough for students to draw on. It is helpful to have the petals and centers cut before the retreat begins.

Hectic Pace or Sacred Space

Too often our lives move at such a fast pace we find no room left for the pursuits that feed our spirits. This retreat is intended to help participants slow down long enough to consider what is getting left out when their lives become unbalanced by busy-ness. It will also introduce them to spiritual practices with which they may not be familiar and/or affirm those in which they already engage. Additionally, it will help participants see how daily demands often cause us to set aside that which is most important—time for journaling, time for prayer, time to just be in the presence of God.

Art supplies and other materials: Materials for "Big Rocks" (see chapter 6), flip chart, markers, pens, paper and any materials required for other activities chosen for this retreat.

Subthemes:
- Slowing down and making room for God
- Seeking God in journaling (activity: rewrite Psalm 23 using your own metaphor)
- Seeking God in nature
- Seeking God in silence
- Seeking God in creation (art activity)
- Seeking God in college life/taking God home

For the first session of this retreat ask participants to introduce themselves. Once that is done, engage them in a discussion
of their images of God and ways in which they have come to
know God—through Scripture, various faith traditions, nature,
thinking about God (i.e., using their reason), relationships with
other people, or other experiences. It is important to be very open-
minded in leading this discussion and allowing students "safe
space" in which to tell their stories. I have found that some of my
students have had some amazing experiences that they seldom talk
about because they are so unusual. I do not think this circumstance is limited to college students. I think many people around
the world have had experiences of the Divine, and many in our
culture are among them.[1] But in twenty-first century U.S. culture,
it is generally unacceptable to discuss such experiences. Scriptures
which may prove useful in this discussion include Psalm 84:11,
Psalm 61:3–4, Psalm 68:5, Isaiah 42:14, and Psalm 23.

Another aspect of this session would be to talk about tran-
scendence and immanence and ask students if God is either or
both. I have found Psalm 139 helpful here for the psalmist writes
that there is no place he can go where God is not present.

The "big rocks" demonstration outlined in chapter 6 might
also be included in this first session. Additionally, the retreat leader
might find it helpful to brainstorm with the students the ways in
which they make room for God in their lives. Ideas might include
time, prayer, silence, dialogue, centering, meditation, journaling,
fasting, drawing, painting, sculpting, writing poetry, experiencing
nature, practicing awareness, using their imaginations, etc.

"Seeking God in Journaling" can be a useful session in this retreat
as a way to get students to focus on slowing down. The retreat facilitator might lead a discussion of Psalm 23, specifically focusing on
God's soothing/slowing down actions: "He *makes me lie down* in
green pastures; he leads me beside *still* waters; he *restores* my soul."
Sometimes students have found it an interesting and enticing exercise to rewrite this psalm in their own metaphor. One of my students
who was in the college wind ensemble wrote about God as her con-
ductor who helped her not to rush the rhythms of her life.

The retreat theme of "Hectic Pace or Sacred Space" lends itself
nicely to making collages. It is fairly easy to find pictures of fast-

paced and leisurely activities in magazines. Having students take time to create collages on this theme often generates new awareness of ways in which they might manage to slow down and make more room for God.

I have included six subthemes for this retreat because some of them can be explored in a relatively short time. For example, while I might thrive on an entire afternoon of silence, it has been my experience that more than one-to-two hours of it will drive most students to the edge of their tolerance. This speaks to me of the outrageous levels of noise we live with in our society, noise that becomes the background for a hectic pace. It is important to understand just how noisy life is for many students. Some of them even have trouble sleeping the first night of a retreat because the retreat environment is too quiet.

"Seeking God in Nature" could involve a group hike, collecting leaves or rocks, bird watching, etc. If the retreat is in a natural setting, unless the weather just absolutely precludes any outdoor activity, it is important to take advantage of the outdoors. This may be one of the few opportunities for intentional experience of nature during the students' college years.

"Seeking God in College Life" would involve a discussion of ways students have made room for God—or not—since they came to school. Many find their newfound freedom from direct parental supervision includes sleeping in on Sunday mornings rather than attending worship. Some students may have connected with one or more faith fellowship groups on campus or at a local church. Some may have come on this retreat precisely because they have not been able to make a connection with God anyplace else in their day-to-day college existence. This discussion period could also provide a time to brainstorm on ways students might take God back to school with them—keeping in mind that God, in my opinion, is already there, but students' need to pay attention and be more aware of God's abiding presence.

Remembering Our Stories

As noted in the outline for "Hectic Pace or Sacred Space," we too often fail to set aside time for reflection in our lives. This retreat is intended to offer participants time to reflect on their personal stories, remembering who they are and whose they are. It also uses stories from various faith traditions to help participants see their stories as part of the larger story of Creation.

Art supplies and other materials: CD Player, David Haas's CD album *You Are Mine*,[2] a CD with quiet piano or guitar music, pencils or pens, plain white paper, 11" x 14" poster board, colored markers, craypas, paper towels, a large compass or plate to use in making a circle on the poster board, Bibles and other sacred texts, resource books.

Subthemes:
- Common Ground: Faith Stories and Our Stories
- Reconnecting
- Stepping Stones
- The Stories We Hold
- Drawing from Memory
- Reflections

Set the stage for this retreat by talking about storytelling being a part of human nature. When we tell stories we create a time apart—time out of time, as it were—somehow suspending natural laws as the words of the story draw us into their world. Stories evoke our emotions—laughter, tears, fear, anger, sorrow, joy, relief, amazement, etc. Susan Albert suggests that

> our lives are made of story: stories handed down from our parents, stories we have created out of our experience, stories about our lives, our work, our explorations, our joys, our disappointments, our learnings—the soul's story. Creating story, we create and re-create ourselves, finding our sacred place in the world of human dreams and achievements on the green earth we inhabit with our fellow human beings.[3]

In the opening portion of this retreat it is important to achieve a mutual understanding that storytelling time is sacred time. It is time to listen to one another. It is time to hear one another on a deeper level than we usually manage to accomplish.

Because some personal stories are difficult to share, it is also important to create an atmosphere of trust and confidentiality, a safe space in which to share both laughter and tears. One of the ways to begin establishing such an atmosphere is through self-introductions in which the participants share their names, why they have come, and where they were born. Just these few simple, personal details will begin the process of reflecting on their own stories. After self introductions the retreat facilitator might invite participants to reflect on the powerful role personal memories play when we take intentional time to reconnect with them. The following poem is the result of such a reflection:

Balloons[4]

Memories rise like bright balloons
riding mind-born winds,
carrying the many selves I've been
across eternity.

Each a part of me no longer known,
they have no strings attached to haul them down
that I might touch their secrets.

Like kaleidoscopes, they change
as recollections fade,
and I cannot remember what I knew.

But memories know . . .
and beckon me to go where they have been;
to know again who it is I am;
to share their freedom, riding on the wind.

David Haas's *"Song of the Body of Christ"* which begins "We come to share our stories, we come to break the bread, we come to know our rising from the dead . . ."[5] is a very appropriate song to sing at this retreat. Obviously it is a Christian song using a decidedly Christian metaphor—thus, for use at a multifaith retreat, it bears a word of explanation for non-Christian students. It could be useful to tell retreatants that the music for the song is based on an ancient Hawaiian tune called *"No Ke Ano Ahi Ahi"* which means "We come to share our stories."[6] It would also be appropriate (and important) to acknowledge that for Christians the images of breaking bread and rising from the dead easily awaken memories of sharing communion and the resurrection of Jesus. Additionally, the retreat facilitator could explain that breaking bread together is one of the most common forms of community known to humankind and that many religions include resurrection stories and a belief in life after death. For example, in Native American culture there is the idea that one remains alive after physical death as long as anyone remembers his or her story.[7]

It is helpful to begin the sharing of stories by reading a tale from the Bible or other sacred text. I have found chapter 1 of the Book of Ruth to be useful here. Another possibility, particularly for a multifaith retreat, would be the story of Hagar and Ishmael in the Book of Genesis. Before the reading, it is a good idea to introduce the idea of "speed bumps" from the *Roadmap for Biblical Interpretation* (see Appendix F), so students can take note of them as the story is read. During the discussion that will follow the reading it is important to encourage students to connect their "speed bumps" to the experiences in their own lives that may have caused them to pause in these places. Using a biblical story like this is an excellent way to create a nonthreatening opening for students to share parts of their stories. Further, as stories are shared, we begin to recognize our own story in the stories of others, an experience that draws us into deeper relationship. Susan Albert agrees:

> Gradually, as we all join in the storytelling, it becomes clear that each story is our story. We do not need to say much, only a few brief words to make the necessary connections. "I've been there too" is a phrase we often hear, and we recognize it as a merging of one story with another. We share laughter, which sometimes helps to puncture our self-inflated selves. We share tears, which come when we are left without words. Both the laughter and the tears are graces, shared emotions, shared compassions. They remind us that ours is a common journey.[8]

Preparatory to bringing this first session to a close, have the students list additional familiar stories from their faith traditions while you or someone else writes them on a flip chart. Then ask the students to think overnight about the stories they chose, why they found them memorable, and why they did or did not like these stories. Leave the list in a place where they can continue to refer to it if they wish.

The opening session for Saturday ("Reconnecting") is intended to reconnect students to the place where things left off the evening before. Go back to the flip chart, and let the participants talk about the ideas that occurred to them overnight regarding these stories. When this discussion seems complete, ask everyone to choose their favorite faith story and imagine themselves as one of the characters, thinking about what they would be doing, what they would be wearing, who their family members would be, etc. Then give participants time to journal about being this character. If the retreat is in a setting that gives them room to wander outdoors, students should feel free to do so, but the facilitator might suggest that they avoid talking to one another in order to maintain an atmosphere conducive to creative writing. After twenty to thirty minutes, the facilitator should call the group back together and let those who wish to do so share what they wrote and/or tell the rest of the group what they gained from this experience.

Another activity that could be added to the morning is creation of life "maps." Using colored markers and plain white paper, ask participants to think about the really major events that have occurred so far in their lives. Tell them to think of these events as "stepping stones," for they are the events that helped students (or caused students) to step from one "place" or level of maturity to another. Explain that once their lists of stepping stones are completed, they are to use the art materials on the tables to represent the events as stones along a path or river, drawing them, labeling them, decorating them however they wish as they "map" their lives. As you bring this activity to a close, allow time for those who want to do so to describe their maps to the group. You might also want to ask them to consider where (or if) they see God's presence in these major events.

The first part of the afternoon should be free-time during which students can nap, do homework, take a walk in the woods, or whatever. In midafternoon, everyone gathers for "The Stories We Hold." It should be obvious to retreatants by now that they have stories within themselves, portions of which have come out in the previous sessions. Now they should be invited to remember a particularly special time and take ten minutes to write about it. This may seem a rather abbreviated period of time. However, the point is not to describe it in detail but to have students reconnect with a particularly fond memory.

At the end of ten minutes, break the group into smaller groups—pairs or triads (whatever one thinks will work best for one's particular students). Have the students share their writings with one another. Then, ask each participant to draw a circle around their favorite sentence in what they wrote about their special memory. They may object that they do not have one favorite sentence or that one sentence cannot be understood apart from the rest of the piece. If this resistance is present, gently suggest that the students do not yet know what the next step is. Invite them to have a bit of trust and do what has been asked anyway. If they feel they need help, they should feel free to call on the other person(s) in their small group for assistance in choosing a single sentence.

When everyone has their sentence, bring them back into a large circle and tell them that together the group is going to create a "verbal collage" by going around the circle and having each person read their one sentence. The results of this activity are usually astounding and sometimes include some really poignant or really hilarious juxtapositions of thoughts. Once everyone has contributed to the group poem, it is important to conclude with a discussion that helps students reflect on the beauty, humor, sadness, or whatever else emerged from weaving a single thought from each of their stories into this group exercise. It might also be useful to ask students if the special memory they chose was among the "stepping stones" they drew on their life maps. If it was not, they might want to consider whether or not it should be added to the map.

The evening session, "Drawing from Memory," will involve the creation of mandalas. The retreat facilitator may need to explain to students what a mandala is (see chapter 8). Give each person a piece of poster board and have them draw a circle more or less in the center of it. Explain that while mandalas are circular in nature, there are no rules for creating them. The students are not "required" to stay within the confines of the circle if they have a need to color/draw outside of it.

Once everyone has drawn their circle, and everyone has access to craypas (we usually share a box between two people), they may not be quite ready to begin—the paper and circle sometimes intimidate the "nonartists" in a group. So tell them that before they begin they might find it helpful to think about symbols that are particularly meaningful to them or which represent one or more of the stepping stones on their life maps.

I have found it useful in this regard to begin mandala sessions with a guided meditation. If you decide to do this, it is important to explain the process to participants, especially for those who have not previously experienced this sort of centering activity. Be sure to let them know they are free to disengage from the meditation at any time if they feel the need to do so. Also let them know they do not need to "move on" in the meditation when the leader suggests that they do so if they are not finished with the "place" where they are when the suggestion is made. I usually make up a meditation that involves going to a quiet place of each participant's choosing such as a meadow or seashore, walking along a path or down a beach, and finding an object that has been left for them by a dear friend or relative. (Note: if all of the participants are Christian, the leader might suggest that the object was left by Jesus.)

Following final instructions on the mandalas, or following the guided meditation if one is used, start some quiet instrumental music on the CD player. This seems to be helpful to the creative process because it creates a certain atmosphere—and, without the music, conversations often begin, creating a noise level that is quite distracting. The music does not inhibit conversation so much as it encourages students to talk in softer tones.

For the closing session on Sunday (or the final day of the retreat if it is not held over a weekend), have the students bring a favorite scripture or other reading that reflects what the students have gotten from the retreat. It is wise for the retreat leader to bring along a variety of resource books that students should be encouraged to explore throughout the retreat such that the need to come up with something for Sunday morning does not feel like a homework assignment on Saturday night. Alternatively, there may be several students who would like to plan the closing session/service/ceremony for everyone else.

At the final session of retreats, as noted earlier, it has been my practice to give my students some small gift to take home in addition to their individual creations. Whether or not this is done will depend in part on whether or not one has the budget to pay for it. Appropriate gifts for "Remembering Our Stories" might include a small journal or blank book, a special pencil or pen, a colorful stone to remind participants of their stepping stones, or some other inexpensive item (OrientalTrading.com is an excellent inexpensive resource for these things).

Other activities that lend themselves to this retreat theme are acrostic poetry writing, mask making, and creating God's eyes (see chapter 8). Books the retreat leader might find useful in preparing for this retreat and/or to include as resources for participants during the retreat are listed in Appendix H.

Other Retreats

By now the potential retreat leader should have a fairly good grasp of how to put together a retreat and break it down into sessions of varying lengths some of which will engage students in Bible study, some in creative arts activities, and some in various spiritual disciplines such as prayer, journaling, and silence. Thus, in this section I shall simply list additional retreat titles and subthemes along with some resources I have used with my students at these events.

Finding Wonder in Winter

- What is "winter?" (Is it more than a season?)
- Winter and Wonder (collages or other activity to highlight wonder in winter)
- Winter Stories (share favorite memories of winter)
- Winter Games (make snow sculptures, play games that involve trails in the snow, or if there is no snow, take a hike or go bird watching; if it is too cold to go outdoors, figure out some indoor games or "ice breakers")

- Cutting Up the Day (make snowflakes)
- The Light of God in Winter (get some inexpensive "stained glass" kits and make sun catchers)

Wake-Up Moments: Paying Attention to God

- Our Spiritual Selves: getting acquainted
- Creating Sacred Space (students gather natural materials or things they find in the stuff they've brought to create a worship center)
- Remembering Wake-Ups (create some art—a drawing, painting, or poem—that illustrates a time when God tried to enter your awareness)
- Awakening to Memories: Sharing Our Wisdom (students share their art and the stories that go with it)
- Seeing Ourselves as God Sees Us (this is a great time to make God's Eyes and/or to have students rewrite the Twenty-Third Psalm in their own metaphor)

Be Still and Know

- Finding Stillness in the Midst of Chaos
- The Stillness of Structure that Gives Birth to Creativity (This can be any sort of creative activity that offers a structure to help students focus—
- Acrostic poetry, collages on the theme of stillness, mandalas, psalm-writing, etc.)
- Making Cloaks of Stillness (dyeing prayer shawls)
- Creating Stillness with Words and Symbols (decorating prayer shawls)
- Finding God in the Stillness (this may be the closing session or it may be a journaling activity; it could even be a silent nature hike)

Into the Woods: A Getaway with God

- Making Connections (Web of Life activity [see chapter 8] followed by creation of nature masks

- Painting Prayers (give students water colors and brushes and invite them to paint one or more prayers)
- Finding a Voice (imagining themselves as the part of nature for which they created a mask, students write out a statement to read at a Council of All Beings to be held later in the retreat)
- Nature Speaks: Council of All Beings (see chapter 8)
- Celebrating the Gift of Creation and God's Love for All

EIGHT

Creative Arts and Activities for Retreats

This chapter is intended as a resource for retreat planners and other educators. While it offers a variety of creative arts and other activities, the ideas included here are by no means an exhaustive list of the possibilities available. I am constantly on the lookout for additional ideas that might engage student imaginations and help them connect with the Sacred. May the suggestions offered here invite you, the reader, to keep your eyes open for new possibilities as well. It is also my hope that these ideas will encourage you to use your own imagination to adapt, modify, and create entirely new activities for use with your students.

Acrostic Poetry Writing

- Flip chart or dry erase board
- Marker
- Paper for each participant
- Pen or pencil for each participant

Step 1—Determine the word that will be used to form the acrostic poem. If your group is studying particular scriptures, presumably this will be a word that has emerged from the texts.

Step 2—Brainstorm words that begin with each letter of the acrostic word.

Step 3—Choose a word from the resulting lists to begin each line of the poem.

Step 4—Write what emerges.

As an added discipline, you might choose to make the first line one word, the second line two words, and increase the number of words in each subsequent line by one. Or, instead of increasing the number of words, you could increase the number of syllables. The structure of this activity helps participants focus their ideas. It can cause students to juxtapose ideas in ways they would not have thought to try if they were free of the structure. In some ways, this could be thought of as a "verbal collage" with some of the same benefits resulting from the creative process.

Shaping an acrostic poem has an element of play that appeals to young adults. It is quite like playing a game. The brainstorming activity gives them the opportunity to throw out "silly" ideas and laugh together. Laughter and fun help the students to approach the process without considering whether or not they "can do it."

Collages

- Scissors (at least one pair for every two people)
- Glue sticks (at least one stick for every two people)
- Poster board (11" x 14")—at least one per person
- Magazines—good variety; at least three per person—all will be shared by the entire group, but having a sufficient supply per person to begin with avoids stifling creativity.

It is helpful to offer encouragement to students before beginning this activity, particularly if there are participants who have not previously made a collage. Students should be assured that there is no one "right" way to make a collage. Encourage them to enjoy

TABLE 8.1
EXAMPLES OF ACROSTIC POETRY WRITING
USING THE WORD *BELOVED*

List of Brainstormed Words:

Benign	Evolve	Longing	Over	Vend	Door
Brave	Even	Leave	Orb	Vendor	Dare
Be	Event	Leaf	Open	Very	Dive
Boundary	Ever	Long	Offer	Verisimili-	Divine
Broken	Every-	Leisure	Offering	tude	Decrepi-
Blessed	thing	Lower	Only	Veracity	tude
Bravado	Evangelize	Loveless	Overture	Visor	Disclose
Bundle	Entry	Lose	Opening	Vacant	Dear
Burn	Enter	Lost	Official	Vibrate	Darling
Burning	Evoke	Lever	Office	Veer	Donut
Bumble-	Evergreen	Lollygag	Onto	Vision	Disgust
bee	Engine	Lollipop	Off	Vote	Disciple
Between	Ember	Luscious	Oblige	Volume	Discipline
Before	Entourage		Oblong	View	Dove
Blend	Endure		Obliterate	Venture	
	Enduring		Oxidize		
	Encourage				

EXAMPLE 1
Be
Everything you
Long to be
Only remember: Loving your
Vision will lead you beyond
Everything even you have imagined,
    for
Divine inspiration is boundless,
    my beloved one.

EXAMPLE 2
Burning
Embers of
Longing for wisdom
Oxidize my fear; I
Venture forth into waters of
Enduring mystery, baptized
    into communion with
Divine Love who calls me into
    being.

the process as much as whatever the product turns out to be. I have also found it helpful to encourage students to try to cover every part of the poster board on which the collage is created and to allow themselves the freedom to glue images and words at different angles. If I fail to mention these things, some students produce very stiff "collages" which show one image after another, none of them overlapping, and all vertical to the viewer. Unless students free themselves to allow overlapping and angling of images, they cannot experience the insights that emerge when images blend into one another—the very insights that are intended to open their imaginations and create "thin places" through which to see/experience the Divine.

It can also be helpful to remind students of the retreat theme or other specialized focus of the activity. For example, collage making could follow a discussion of a sacred text(s) or a particular topic (prayer, relationships, nature, a season of the year, etc.) Perhaps there is a certain question on which it would be helpful to encourage students to focus such as, "What does it mean to be loved by God?" or "In what ways is God's love for me revealed in my life?"

In a retreat setting, collage making tends to be a group activity engaged in at a large table with stacks of magazines provided. These will include mail-order catalogues, nature magazines, pop-culture magazines, household décor magazines, etc. Sufficient pairs of scissors and glue sticks should be supplied such that no more than two people at a time must share these resources.

I have rarely had a group of students who are silent during collage making, but it never hurts to encourage them to ask one another to keep their eyes open for particular images they may be seeking and to talk with one another as they work. I have found 11" x 14" pieces of poster board to be the most ideal size on which to create collages. This size is large enough to allow room for creative ideas to emerge and is small enough to be inexpensively framed should students choose to preserve their work.

The collage process allows students considerable creative freedom to develop their own understandings of scriptures, topical themes, or questions in a nonthreatening activity (since there is no single "right" way to create a collage). It also helps them process their understandings together through conversations they carry on as they work—again, a nonthreatening way in which to have a discussion. Additionally, collage seems to work at an almost subconscious level to reveal interpretations and relationships between ideas students might not have discovered without graphically juxtaposing them on a piece of poster board. As artist/author Cathy Malchiodi says, "Collage . . . is truly a transformative experience of taking what already exists and finding unexpected associations and meanings by creating a new context."[1]

Through the interpretive process of collage, students often are able to find their "voice" and make connections between their own stories and The Story. Then, when they share their creations with one another, they are all blessed with insights the others bring. Having them work with their hands to actually create a work of art gives them a new tool for exploring and understanding sacred texts, the big questions of life, or even a particular mood or emotion. The process has the additional benefit of communicating across learning styles, visual, kinesthetic, and aural.

Collages resulting from this activity can be inexpensively framed. If one desires to make a more three-dimensional collage, then any of the following might be added to the available materials: beads, yarn, feathers, buttons, leaves, dried flowers, bottle caps, paper clips, etc.

Council of All Beings

But ask the beasts
    and they shall teach you;
and the fowls of the air,
    and they shall teach you;
or speak to the earth,
    and it shall teach you;
and the fishes of the sea
    shall declare unto you.
—Job 12:7–8

This activity helps students to really think about nature in ways they might not previously have considered. Have the students make masks representing some portion of nature that particularly attracts them, holds special meaning for them, or about which they would like to know more (instructions for making masks are included later in this chapter). When the masks are completed, allow time for students to find the "voice" of their part of nature. Have them reflect on what it would be like to be that part of nature and what they would have to say to the rest of creation if they were invited to participate in a council of all beings. As an example, the voice of a mountain stream (as I imagined it) might be offered:

A Mountain Stream Speaks

I am constantly changing,
never the same
as I move between the banks
that shepherd me to the sea.
I flow with the change,
eroding my banks, altering them
as they channel me.
We are integrally part of one another.
I offer my life-giving substance
to the animals of the forest
and the trees and shrubs
that help to hold my banks together
with their strong roots.
I am home to fish, tadpoles,
and other water creatures—
a playground for otters and beavers.
I swell with the gift of rain;
I shrink with the curse of drought;
I am polluted with the trash of humans
who don't seem to care
that I would give life to them as well
if they but kept me clean.
With heavy spring rains
I race to remove the detritus,
carelessly thrown,

washing it away
that I might flow free and clean once more,
bubbling, chuckling, laughing
my way to the sea.

Exploring Nature's Shadows

- Stiff paper at least 11" x 14"
- Pencils or charcoal
- Oil crayons, paint, or other coloring medium

For this activity, ask students to each take a piece of paper and a pencil or stick of charcoal outside and find a place where something in nature can cast its shadow on the paper. Then students will outline the shadow with pencil or charcoal, bring it back to a central place with a table, and paint or color it as they choose. The idea is to make them aware of shadows in a way they may not have been previously. A corollary activity would be to discuss the gifts of shadow—refuge, incubation (seeds in the dark soil, gestation in the darkness of the womb), aids to seeing light (for example, how many of us have ever noticed a firefly or stars during the daytime?). In ancient times we are told people went into the streets just to have Peter's shadow fall on them with its healing power.[2]

God's Eyes

- Different colored skeins of yarn
- Scissors
- Two sticks per person—sticks should be of equal length, at least 10 inches long, and relatively straight

God's eyes are a simple craft that appeals to students because it produces bright objects with which to decorate their residence hall rooms while reminding them of the setting in which they were created. Generally, I use this activity on retreats at which we have discussed the possibility that God does not "see" through human eyes.

I first came up with this distinction in the early 1990s when I was teaching an adult Sunday school class at a church in mid-Missouri. The class had been struggling with concepts of Divine judgment and grace. During the following week, as I thought about the ideas various class members had expressed, it occurred to me that the confusion was arising because we were attributing human characteristics to God. Even the list below (see figure 8.1) is obviously an anthropomorphization of the Divine, but I have found it helps my college students to think about these ideas in a new way.

FIGURE 8.1
HUMAN JUDGMENT VS. DIVINE JUDGMENT

Human judgment is often based on:	*Divine judgment is ALWAYS based on:*
• injured pride	• love
• prejudice	• full knowledge of all
• jealousy	circumstances
• envy	• understanding
• contempt	• mercy
• intolerance	• compassion
• self-conceit	
• insensitive or deliberate ignorance	

When we think of *judgment*, we tend to think of it in human terms. It is no wonder we then fear a judgmental God.

To make a God's eye, begin by fastening two sticks together at right angles by winding yarn around them at their approximate centers. Then begin to wrap the sticks with yarn in concentric squares, winding the yarn once around a stick, moving to the next, winding the yarn once around that stick, moving to the next, and so forth. The yarn is applied in a single layer, moving from the center of each "arm" of the God's eye to the outside. There are several ways in which the pattern may be varied, including twisting two different colors of yarn together and winding them as one strand. One can make the design more three-dimensional by alternating the direction from which one wraps each stick. Experiment! It's only yarn and sticks—you can always unwind it and start over if you wish. Like so many artistic endeavors, there is no single "right" way to do this.

Ink and Craypas Drawings[3]

- Stiff paper at least 11" x 14"—bring enough for each student to have *at least* two pieces
- Chalks or oil pastels
- Newspaper
- Black Ink (preferably water-soluble)
- Cotton string or yarn cut in 18-inch lengths

This activity is designed to tap one's inner source of spontaneous imagery. It is best to work on a flat surface, covered with newspaper, because the ink might run. It is also wise to wear old clothing, even if the ink being used is water-soluble. Saturate the string with ink, then use the soaked string to make lines and shapes on the paper. Using different movements will result in different lines, shapes, and spots. Once you have had enough of slinging ink, let the ink dry. Then turn the paper to view it from different angles. What shapes or objects appear? Use the chalks or oil pastels to bring out these images. Encouraging students to give their drawings a title can bring them further illumination as to what they are seeing. Using this activity as a follow-up to a discussion about their spiritual lives and growing closer to the Divine often influences what comes out of these drawings.

Mandalas

- Oil crayons
- Poster board (11" x 14")—at least one per person
- Paper towels or rags
- Compass or round plate at least 10" in diameter
- Drawing tools such as rulers, French curves, and protractors

Circular designs, often geometric, are found in cultures around the world, many of which revere the circle as a powerful symbol.

Mandala is a Sanskrit word for "Magic Circle."[4] Their creation has been a part of human spiritual practice for thousands of years. Examples of circular sacred sites include the circular labyrinth at France's Chartres Cathedral, created in the thirteenth century, and the prehistoric Stonehenge monument in Wiltshire, England.

"Mandala drawing . . . has been used both for finding one's spiritual center and for reflection on the nature of existence."[5] The circle is merely a place to begin; it should not be permitted to limit one's imagination. Sometimes it is important to let oneself draw outside the lines to fill the entire page, or to decorate the circular design beyond the limits of the circle itself, letting whatever seems to belong be included. Allowing oneself the freedom to remember there is no right way to do this project is one key to allowing spiritual insight to emerge.

Masks

- Large paper bags
- Scissors
- Felt scraps
- Cotton balls/colored yarn balls
- Crayons
- Paint
- Colored pipe cleaners
- Glue
- Leaves
- Feathers

Mask making offers all sorts of possibilities from initiating a discussion of the cultural and psychological "masks" virtually everyone wears to making props for interpretation of a sacred text or for "becoming" someone or something else in order to imagine life from that person's or other thing's point of view. The event at which mask making came into play for my students was our retreat "Into the Woods: A Getaway with God" at which we held a "Council of All Beings." In order to "become" these beings, we made masks to represent our new personas. This same activity could easily become a part of the retreat "Celebration of Creation" as well.

Materials for masks are not limited to those I have listed. Depending on the theme and purpose of the masks, other materials might be included. The only limit to this activity is one's imagination.

Painting Prayers

- Watercolor paper
- Watercolor paint
- Cups or bowls to hold water
- Paint brushes

When we are children we play with creative things like watercolors and finger paints whenever the opportunity arises, even if our "paint" is a mixture of water and dirt. Students' eyes light up with anticipation when they enter a room in which watercolor tins and brushes have been placed on tables.

To begin this activity, engage students in a discussion of prayer. What are some of the prayer forms they have tried? Have they ever just sat listening for God rather than doing all the talking themselves? Let them know there are many ways to pray, including taking a mindful walk in the woods or writing in one's journal. Then ask them to consider what a prayer might look like if it were painted. Would it include words or not? What images might it offer to God? Perhaps it would be an array of color in no particular pattern. Listen to their ideas if they choose to voice them. Then invite them to paint a prayer.

Prayer Beads

- 28 small beads per person (8 mm)
- 4 larger beads per person (10 mm)
- 1 invitatory bead per person (10 mm or 12 mm)
- 1 faith symbol per person (cross, fish, ark, Star of David, etc.)
- 36 to 70 spacer beads per person (the larger variety of "seed beads")
- 28 gauge or smaller jeweler's wire (the higher the number, the smaller the wire) I have found 28 gauge seems to work best for

my students; thicker wire is too stiff and thinner wire tends to break too easily.

Prayer beads, or rosaries, can be traced as far back as the eighth century BCE and can be found in every major religion. All prayer beads have a common purpose—they are intended as an aid to meditation and/or contemplation. Fingering the beads helps one stay focused on one's prayers. To this end, most prayer beads are made of similarly shaped beads of wood, stone, or other sturdy materials. Repetition of prayers serves to focus one's attention on God and open space for communication with God by minimizing distractions. The beads I have made with my students consist of four groups of seven beads (see figure 8.2). These groups may represent many things—four weeks, four seasons, four directions.

Gathering Materials: The wire can be cut into 30- to 36-inch lengths using scissors. Give each participant a wire and have him or her choose the beads they want to use. It is helpful to temporarily secure a bead to one end of the wire by looping the wire through the bead and wrapping the short end once or twice around the wire on which you will be stringing the rest of the beads.

Stringing the Beads: Begin stringing with the large bead (10 mm) shown at the bottom of the diagram in figure 8.2. Add one, two, or even three small seed beads. Then add one of the 8 mm beads, one or two more seed beads, another 8 mm bead, seed bead(s), etc., following the pattern of the diagram. When you have finished stringing all the beads in the circle, pass the wire back through the first large (10 mm) bead parallel to the other end of the wire. You should now have a ring of beads with two wires sticking out of the connecting bead in the same direction. Slide the ring of beads to the approximate center of the wire and even up the two ends. Then, using both ends as one wire, pass them through two or three seed beads, the invitatory bead (which can be the same as the larger beads in the circle or as different as your supplies of beads allow), and two or three more seed beads.

To add the faith symbol, separate the two wires and pass one through each end of the symbol in *opposite* directions (i.e., if you have a cross with a loop on top, for example, pass each end of the wire through the loop in *opposite* directions) and pull the wire

FIGURE 8.2
PRAYER BEAD PATTERN

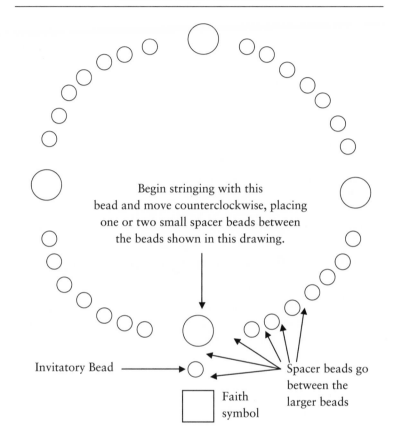

Begin stringing with this
bead and move counterclockwise, placing
one or two small spacer beads between
the beads shown in this drawing.

Invitatory Bead

Faith
symbol

Spacer beads go
between the
larger beads

firmly but not so tightly that you will not be able to perform the
next task. This next task is the part my students and I find the
most challenging.

Once you have secured the faith symbol, pass BOTH wires
back up through the seed beads, the invitatory bead, seed beads
and first 10 mm bead. At the top of the 10 mm bead, you should
have beads on single wires going in two directions. Feed one end
of the double wire you've just emerged with through as many

beads as you are able on one side; do the same on the other side with the other end of the double wire. Then clip whatever wire is sticking out as closely as you can.

Praying with the Beads: When praying privately, the prayers assigned to each bead are up to the individual who is praying.

- Plan what thoughts or prayers you wish to assign each bead. Memorize the words.
- Find the right time and place so you can work through the beads at an unhurried pace. Find a place that is quiet and where you can be undisturbed.
- Start and end with a moment of silence. Get centered; taking a couple of deep breaths may help. Prepare to focus on your meditation.
- Hold the faith symbol and begin to pray.
- Move to the invitatory bead; pray the prayer you have assigned it.
- Enter the circle of prayer, saying the prayer for each bead.
- Close your prayers and conclude with a moment of silence.

When praying the beads in a group, it is important to all use the same prayers. Possible prayers for individual or group use might be based on the Psalms. As an example:

Praying around the Circle:

Invitatory: "Let the words of my mouth and the meditation of my heart be acceptable to you, O LORD, my rock and my redeemer." —Psalm 19:14

Large Beads: "Be still and know that I am God."—Psalm 46:10

Small Beads: "Bless the LORD, O my soul, and all that is within me bless God's holy name."—Psalm 103:1

Prayer Rocks

- Flat rocks from a garden shop or other source (dark-colored or black are best)
- Marker pens that write in white, gold, or silver

Students are invited to choose a rock and write a one- or two-word prayer concern on it and leave it on an altar or place it on a worship center. Some students will include drawings as part of their prayers. The rocks may be left for the entire retreat or only for a specific session. Students may want to make multiple rocks as more prayers occur to them during the retreat. The rocks should be available for students to take with them at the end of the retreat.

Prayer Shawls

- Scissors (at least one pair for every two people)
- Poster board—any size—for making cut out shapes
- Muslin—One piece 18" x 72" per person
- Spray-on Fabric Dye
- Bucket or pan of water
- Paper
- Pens
- Fabric paint
- Paper towels
- Sponges to cut into shapes or pre-cut sponges (optional)
- Paint brushes (optional)
- Tables
- Plastic drop cloths to cover tables
- Macramé cord
- Thread & sewing needles

Making prayer shawls gives students a great deal of freedom in creating wearable art that will remind them of the retreat on which it was created and will hopefully encourage them to engage in prayer more often than they might have otherwise. It also gives them the freedom to engage in biblical interpretation in a non-threatening, fun activity.

Prayer implies communication and connection—that is between the one who is praying and the one to whom the prayer is directed. Major ideas that recur in the retreats I conduct with students are God's love for us, our belonging to God, God's presence with us, and our chosenness—that is, relationship. Prayer is something that helps make us conscious of God's presence and our belovedness. Therefore, creating prayer shawls is an activity appropriate to many of the retreats I have outlined in chapters 6 and 7.

Dyeing process: Begin with a strip of white muslin, 72" x 18" (36"-wide muslin cut into 2-yard lengths and then ripped in half down the center *lengthwise*). Wet the muslin in a bucket of water and ring it out until the muslin is merely damp. Spread it on the ground outside (in case of rain, the dyeing can be accomplished indoors on plastic drop cloths). Apply dyes from spray bottles. The dyes I have found to work best are "Tumble-Dye" brand available from Hobby Lobby or online at www.craftsetc.com. (Just type "Fabric Dye" into the page's search box and the dyes should pop right up.) The advantages of using these dyes include not needing to apply a fixative and their ease of application. If desired, you may place flat objects on the shawls to create silhouettes—leaves work well. Also, you might cut out objects (or letters) from poster board. (Paper will work, but poster board stands up better when it gets wet.) The muslin may also be "bunched" to create places where the dye is not sprayed. You may choose to spray a different color of dye on the white spaces left by the flat objects (or "bunching"). Once the dyeing is completed, the shawls are hung in trees or spread on bushes to dry. (Drying generally takes one to two hours, depending on the relative humidity of the day.)

Painting process: Fabric paints in varying colors and finishes (matte, metallic, shiny, glitter) may be used. Before painting, look at the dyed fabric to see if there are any shapes or images that seem to have happened by chance in the dyeing process. These could be highlighted with paint. A favorite quotation or text might also be written in paint on the shawl. What symbols are especially meaningful that might be drawn using paint? A sponge could also be cut into a shape, then used to "stamp" paint onto the shawl. Paint can be applied from the bottles, brushed on, put on with fingers, spread out after application using brushes or fingers, etc. There is no single "right way" to do this. The paint will need to dry for about six hours.

Finishing: Once the dyeing and painting processes are completed, sew a piece of macramé cord to each corner. These pieces are about 12" long and serve to give the shawls a more finished appearance. They are also useful if one wishes to hang the shawl on a wall. Other decorations can also be added once the paint is dry—buttons, beads, feathers, etc., can all be sewn onto the shawl.

Web of Life

- A large ball of yarn
- Index cards on which are written various parts of nature

For this activity the facilitator will need to imagine various parts of nature. Possibilities include the forest, a lake, a river, a fish, a bird, a bear, an owl, a woodpecker, fire, an earthworm, grass, a coyote, a bobcat, a deer, a rabbit, a turtle, a flower, a meadow, a bush, earth, etc.

Each student is given an index card to indicate his or her role in this activity. Hand the yarn to one of the students who has a card indicating he/she is an animal. Instruct the student to hold on to the loose end of the yarn before throwing the ball itself to the student whom you will indicate.

When that instruction seems clear, suggest that the animal goes to the lake to get a drink. The person who starts the yarn will hold onto the loose end and toss the ball to the lake. The lake might throw it to the fish, again holding on to the yarn as the ball itself is passed on. The fish might leap up to catch a bug and notice a flower growing at the edge of the lake—so the fish throws the ball to the flower . . . and a web begins to form. The flower sees the rabbit coming to make a salad out of it, the rabbit becomes dinner for the coyote, the coyote runs to the lake for a drink. However this goes, it has been my experience that animals come to the lake a lot, so many strands of the web are tied to the lake. When the web is sufficiently woven, ask students what will happen if the lake becomes polluted. Let them think about it for a moment and then instruct the lake to let go of all the strands he/she is holding. The web, of course, collapses.

This sounds really simple—yet every time I have used it with students, they have let out audible gasps when they see the extent of the damage to the web they have created that results from the destruction of one important portion. This helps them connect to ecological crises in ways merely reading about such problems never can. This activity can also lead to a discussion of students' spiritual lives by noting how integral spiritual nurture is to human well-being and suggesting that failure to care for one's spirit is as personally destructive as failure to care for a water source can be in the environment.

Insights, Understandings, and Recommendations

*The place God calls you to is the place where your deep
gladness and the world's deep hunger meet.*

—Frederick Buechner

Long before I became a college chaplain in August 1997, personal retreats were a significant part of my efforts to care for my own spiritual well-being. When I came to the college I serve, I discovered very little in the way of organized religious and spiritual life activities for the students. In the 1996–1997 academic year, there had been a chaplain intern on campus for ten months, a student from Louisville Theological Seminary who went back to Louisville at the end of her internship. Prior to her coming, the college had been without a chaplain for nearly a decade.

One of the activities the chaplain intern had initiated during her ten-month stay was a midwinter spiritual life retreat at a church camp two-and-one-half hours north of the campus. I knew, after talking with the students who had participated the previous year, that this was an event I wanted to continue to offer. In February 1998, four students and I went to the camp for a retreat. Our theme was "Where is God at college?"

143

Insights and Understandings

On that first retreat, I gained two significant understandings: 1) that students relax in a retreat setting and talk more easily about their deep desires and spiritual longings than they do during fellowship meetings on campus and 2) that it is important to provide retreat opportunities even if only a few students choose to participate because it offers those who attend a chance to encounter intentional time-out-of-time in a way that is not available to them in any other part of their college experience.

In February of the following year, 1999, I took ten students to the same place for a retreat on the theme, "Hectic Pace or Sacred Space?" The previous year, all four students had been Christians. For this second retreat, a Buddhist, a Wiccan, and an Agnostic were among the attendees. The increased numbers and more diverse religious backgrounds definitely changed the dynamics of the group, but the depth of meaningful experience remained, an assessment I infer from the eagerness of many of these same students to help organize and plan the retreat in February 2000.

During those initial retreat experiences, writing a book about planning and leading spiritual retreats for college students was beyond my wildest imaginings. Consequently, I have no formal assessments of the students' experiences on the early retreats, as I had not yet realized the benefits of written evaluations in planning subsequent events. I thought the students' verbal feedback was sufficient, not having become conscious of the fact that students will say much more anonymously on a written evaluation than they are apt to say face-to-face with the retreat facilitator.

Spiritual retreats are a new idea to many students. They are attracted to them as an adventure away from campus, an adventure to which they must commit their time, but one that does not place an additional strain on the already overstretched finances from which most of my students seem to suffer.

In my early years in campus ministry, I would program almost every minute of our weekend retreats. However, I have learned that this is not wise. Sometimes activities take longer than expected; sometimes students need more free time to explore the natural environment in which the retreat is held or to engage in significant conversations that emerge from being in a retreat setting. Without flexibility built into the schedule, opportunities for adjusting to these circumstances are erased.

Like most of us, students appreciate being needed. They are eager to help. The generation of students now entering college has been dubbed "the millennials." In his discussion of the characteristics of this generation, Robert DeBard noted that they are team-oriented, they like to work on projects together, and they have been raised to appreciate structure.[1] These characteristics mean students appreciate being asked to help plan and carry out retreats—as long as there is a "safety net" of structure that prevents their risking failure—for another characteristic of millennials is their need for approval. "Millennial students feel pressured to perform; they want a structure enforced to ensure that compliance will lead to achievement."[2]

Another important understanding is that every retreat is different. Even if I were to offer the same theme and activities on every retreat in the same place, and even if the students who attended were the same group every time we went, none of us would be the persons we had been six to twelve months earlier. Every one of us would bring months of new life experience to each subsequent event. Of course, I offer students different themes for each retreat, and the students who attend are a mixture of seasoned veterans and persons for whom a spiritual retreat is a brand new experience.

After our retreat in February 2000, a number of students expressed a desire to have one in the fall semester as well. I had mixed feelings about that, wondering if offering two retreats each year might not diminish the depth of experience wrought by scarcity and anticipation. As it turns out, my concerns were unfounded. Holding a retreat each semester has opened up the opportunity to participate for more students who for one reason or another might not have been available on the third weekend in February, the time we have traditionally held our midwinter event. Holding two retreats each year has also doubled the opportunities for students who are particularly drawn to retreats to have multiple experiences of them during their years at college.

Recommendations for Offering
Retreats at Other Institutions

This topic was addressed in some detail in the portion of chapter 5 called "Retreat Basics." In summary, to offer a retreat one must have space in which to hold the event, a means of feeding and housing those who attend, transportation to and from the event, a flexible schedule that permits planned and unplanned activities, one or more means of publicizing the event, and a plan for taking care of housekeeping chores like cooking and cleaning up so these tasks are distributed fairly among all the attendees, unless one has a budget to afford catered meals.

Obviously, if one has meals catered by nonparticipants, the overall experience of the participants will change. I have not had the budget to afford this "luxury," and after so many retreat experiences with my students during which we took care of the meals ourselves, I am not sure I would advocate catering. The students enjoy cooking for one another; for some of them, this is their first hands-on kitchen experience. Meal preparation and cleanup, as team efforts, are a primary means of building community among the participants. But whether or not the participants prepare the meals themselves, eating together is an important part of the retreat experience. "Eating and drinking together in all human societies is a primordial act of bonding."[3]

The retreats in chapters 6 and 7 are adaptable to shorter time frames and need not be limited to use with college students. For example, in the spring of 2002, I was invited to Las Cruces, New Mexico, to facilitate a one-day spiritual life event for adults from four congregations in the Tres Rios Conference of the Christian Church (Disciples of Christ). I adapted the retreat schedule to offer two sessions on Saturday morning and two on Saturday afternoon, followed by a closing worship experience, as opposed to one session on Friday evening, three on Saturday, and closing worship on Sunday morning.

The advantage of the Friday night through Sunday morning schedule is that it offers participants more time to "digest" each session, thus deepening their experience. But if one must confine one's schedule to a single day, though the experience of the participants will be different, it is certainly a valid approach to spiritual nurture. If one must choose the one-day format, it is helpful to provide snacks and lunch in ways that do not require the participants to take time in preparation and cleanup (e.g., have pizza delivered for lunch). Even though food preparation and cleanup are community-building activities, the time for the retreat is already shortened by its compaction into a single day. Therefore, should one choose to offer a single-day retreat, determining whether or not time is actually available for meal preparation and cleanup is an important consideration.

Another possible schedule I tried with my students was Friday evening from 6:30 to 10:30 and Saturday morning from 8:30 to 12:30, with two sessions on Friday and two on Saturday. This might have worked if we had taken these retreats off campus. But, motivated by a very limited budget, I scheduled them this way in order to save the costs of housing and transportation.

The problem was that the campus, with all its other activities and distractions, was too easily accessible. Some students came for both Friday night and Saturday morning, but some who came on Friday did not return for the Saturday portions of the event. Worse yet, some of the students who came on Saturday had not been present for the foundational portions of the event on Friday night that led to what was going on during the Saturday segment. All of this shifting of people in and out kept changing the dynamics of the group. We were not able to develop the sense of community that is possible by going off campus and living together for forty-eight hours.

Now and then one will encounter a "problem student" who just wants to be a clown and not take things seriously, or one who is in some other way disruptive to the other participants at a retreat. When this happens, I recommend talking to such students one-on-one hoping to help them see how they are spoiling the retreat/program experience for others. I understand such behavior as a cry for attention—even negative attention can seem better than a perceived lack of attention. Try to ask questions that will help the student understand his/her behavior. Whenever possible, try to give such students a task that bears some responsibility for the success of the program/activity. If the student has a vested interest in a positive outcome, he or she is less likely to be disruptive.

I have been known to tell such students point blank that I see their behavior as a cry for help—help which I am willing to try to provide but they must agree to change their disruptive behavior as we work out the ways in which I might help (including finding them professional counseling or other assistance beyond what I am able to give). When all else fails, as has happened once in my experience, I will tell the student that he or she is barred from attending any future spiritual life retreats until he or she gets the counseling or whatever else is necessary to change his/her disruptive behavior.

Whether a retreat is offered on campus, near campus, in a church building, or at a camp in the woods, it is important to be cognizant of creating atmospheres appropriate to each session. For example, if "Morning Watch" is to be part of the retreat experience, quiet, contemplative music might be playing as participants gather, with no artificial sources of light except for a few candles. A display of rocks, colored leaves, and/or feathers might be arranged on a piece of colorful cloth either on the floor or a table, depending on whether participants will be sitting on chairs or on the floor (or on the ground—some settings lend themselves to holding "Morning Watch" outdoors).

For creative arts activities, my students and I generally prefer to arrange the room in a large ring of tables. (For smaller groups, a couple of tables pushed together to make a single large table is sufficient.) In this situation, one must consider whether the arts activity is meant to be contemplative or interactive. Quiet music and beginning with a guided meditation before creating a mandala, for example, creates a decidedly different atmosphere than a group discussion of the retreat theme followed by the somewhat interactive activity of creating collages from magazine pictures and words. During collage making, students will sometimes shout out requests for particular things such as, "Has anyone run across photos of space or stars?" or "I need penguins! If you see penguins, send them this way!" or "Please pass the glue/scissors" (if there are not enough glue sticks and scissors for each person to have their own).

One of the best pieces of advice I can offer anyone who wants to lead a retreat is to take the time to sit down and think through every part of it from beginning to end. Imagine yourself greeting the participants at the gathering place. Perhaps it is appropriate to offer a prayer for your time together before loading up the vehicles. Think about your arrival. Are there instructions you should give about unloading and getting settled?

What will happen once the group has claimed the retreat space? If dinner is the first activity, who will get the meal ready? Do you have all the utensils and dishes you will need if they are not provided at the site? After dinner, how should the space be arranged for the evening session? Do you have all the materials you will need? Think through the entire retreat in this way, imagining each step of each session and the materials you will need to have on hand for them. Will you need newspaper to cover tables or to help in starting a campfire? Do you have matches? Make a list of materials as you are imagining your way through the retreat—then go collect them as part of your pre-retreat preparations.

It is also extremely wise to have a food checklist, in addition to the planned menu, for use when you are loading the vehicles prior to departure. In the past, I have sent the menu for our retreats over to our food service, gone with students to pick up the food, loaded vehicles, and then discovered upon our arrival that some critical thing has been left behind. One year it was the milk; another year we arrived without any eggs. A sample retreat food checklist, based on the sample menu in Appendix A, is provided in Appendix B.

Some sort of evaluative instrument employed at the end of the retreat can be helpful in determining what worked well, what might be improved, and/or what might be done differently, added, or deleted. It may seem like a hassle to stop in the midst of leave-taking to have students fill out an evaluation, but it is an important part of the process. Written evaluations help participants take some intentional time to reflect on what happened during the weekend and provide feedback to event planners. The students who have just completed a retreat are also a great resource for new ideas, activities, and future retreat themes. The evaluation form I developed for use with my students is provided in Appendix E.

I also encourage those who offer retreats to consider including some sort of creative arts for all the reasons previously outlined. Even planners who do not consider themselves artistic can find new gifts within themselves if they will only get over "I can't" and move to "I shall try." I will never forget my own experience at a Christian Education committee meeting at a church in Missouri in 1988. We were planning a church-wide event called "Celebrating God's Love through the Arts." One idea that came up was to offer each participant the opportunity to paint a segment of glass to create a "stained glass window" on which someone from the committee would have drawn a design in "liquid lead." The committee chair turned to me and said, "Kathleen, I want you to go find the biggest piece of glass that seems reasonable and draw the design." I was horrified! "But . . . but . . . " I sputtered, "I don't draw!" The committee chair calmly looked me in the eye and stated, "Now you do!" I got the glass—it measured 3 feet by 4 feet. I drew a design—an amazing experience. The congregation came to the event and thoroughly enjoyed hands-on participation in making something so lovely. As far as I know, that glass is still displayed in the congregation's fellowship hall.

We may not consider ourselves "artists," but we are all called by God to discover our gifts for cocreation. We must all get over "I can't," in order to discover the surprising joy that comes from creativity. As Cathy Malchiodi notes in her book *The Soul's Palette*, "Art is good for you and may be as important to your overall health as balanced nutrition, regular exercise, or meditation."[4]

Conclusion

It is my hope that the retreat outlines provided in chapters 6 and 7 and the creative arts and other retreat activities detailed in chapter 8 will offer resources for colleges, universities, and seminaries offering training in youth and young adult ministries, as well as for campus ministries and congregations seeking ways to nurture congregational spiritual life. Retreats are a ministry tool that can be used in a broad range of settings. College students are not the only portion of the population to whom such experiences will appeal. These retreats are a tool that can be used with an entire congregation or limited to groups of similar age or interest. At colleges and universities, retreats are a tool that can help create community among students, faculty, and staff—though initially faculty and staff may resist invitations to participate with students in such informal settings. However, in my experience, once faculty and/or staff have participated in a retreat, they are eager to come again.

Several weeks before our retreat in October 2004, the chair of our religious studies department stopped me on the sidewalk to say, "I have some really sad news." All sorts of dire possibilities passed through my mind as I waited for her to continue. "I will not be able to attend the fall spiritual life retreat," she said. She was right; her news was sad—and it was a testament to the value of her prior retreat experiences that she experienced a sense of loss from not being able to participate in this one.

I also hope the retreats I have outlined spur others to develop ideas of their own. As Tom Beaudoin wrote in the late 1990s, "The limits of our ministries are the limits of our imaginations."[5] May your imagination soar and your ministry be blessed!

Sample Retreat Menu

FRIDAY—SUPPER
Sandwiches—white bread and wheat bread
- sliced cheese
- sliced ham OR beef (depending on the faith traditions of your students)
- sliced turkey
- peanut butter
- jelly
- mustard, mayonnaise, ketchup
- pickles

Chips
Raw veggies—carrots, celery, broccoli
Fruit—apples, bananas, oranges
Sodas & Juice
Hot Chocolate
Tea
Cookies
Marshmallows

BOTH MORNINGS FOR BREAKFAST

Eggs
Cheese
Fruit: Apples, Bananas, Oranges
Milk
Butter
Soy Milk
Coffee
Tea
Fruit Juice

Cereal
Bacon—Be sensitive to your
    students' faith traditions
    here!
Toast—white and/or wheat
Jelly

SATURDAY NOON

Grilled cheese sandwiches and tomato soup. (Participants who do
not want grilled cheese can make sandwiches from the ingredients
left over from Friday night.)

SATURDAY NIGHT

Baked Spaghetti (meatless since some participants may be vege-
    tarians)
Baked Lasagna
Parmesan Cheese
Salad
Salad Dressing
Garlic Bread
Sodas & Juice
Cookies

Retreat Food Checklist

_____ Bread (4 meals)

_____ Sliced Cheese (2 meals)

_____ Sliced Turkey (one meal)

_____ Sliced Beef or Ham (one meal)

_____ Peanut Butter

_____ Jelly

_____ Mustard, Mayonnaise, Ketchup

_____ Salad Dressing (1 meal)

_____ Pickles

_____ Chips (3 meals)

_____ Raw Veggies (2 meals)

_____ Fruit—apples, oranges, bananas (4 meals)

_____ Sodas (3 meals)

_____ Milk (5 meals)

_____ Vanilla Soy Milk (2 people)

_____ Tea (2 meals)

_____ Hot Chocolate (4 meals)

_____ Water (5 meals)

_____ Coffee (2 meals)

_____ Fruit Juice (3 meals)

_____ Cookies (3 meals)

_____ Marshmallows (1 meal)

_____ Eggs (2 meals)

_____ Bacon (2 meals) Remember to be sensitive to faith traditions with this food!

_____ Grated Cheddar Cheese (2 meals)

_____ Grated Parmesan Cheese (1 meal)

_____ Bagels (2 meals)

_____ Cream Cheese (2 meals)

_____ Butter (3 meals—including one lunch of grilled cheese sandwiches)

_____ Tomato Soup (1 meal)

_____ Lasagna (½ meal)

_____ Baked Spaghetti (½ meal)

_____ Garlic Bread (1 meal)

_____ Salad (1 meal)

_____ Cereal (2 meals)

Retreat Responsibilities

Responsibility	Fri. PM	Sat. AM	Sat. Noon	Sat. PM	Sun. AM
Make Fire					
Set Tables					
Cook					
Clean Up					
Clean Fireplace					
Clean Kitchen					
Put Away Tables & Chairs					
Sweep & Mop Lodge					

Student Self-Evaluation of Arts Projects (Dance, Drama, Music, Literary, Visual) Produced in the Context of Theological Coursework[1]

Answer the following questions as part of the preparation of your project:

1. With what group of people do you intend to use this work? How do you hope this piece of creative work will address them? What emotional or moral influence do you hope it will have on these persons?

2. Describe the process engaged in to produce the artwork. How does the process relate to the class assignment or content?

3. Explain the choices and decisions that led to the final form presented for evaluation. If you cannot, why not?

4. Indicate clearly how the artwork comes out of the text and is related to it. What is the connection between the artwork itself and the learning that it is supposed to represent?

Retreat Evaluation

Please respond to the following statements to help us plan for future retreats:

1. I decided to attend this retreat because . . .

2. For me, the most meaningful part of this retreat was . . . Why?

3. My spirituality was fed by . . .

4. Additional things that would have fed my spiritual life are . . .

5. I would like to have had more . . .

6. The creative arts activities were . . .

5. I would attend a retreat like this again. _____Yes
   _____No

Roadmap for Biblical Interpretation— Severely Abridged[2]

B ased on a handout by Dr. David Hopkins with notes to self added during a class with Dr. Denise Dombkowski-Hopkins[3]

1. BEGINNING THE JOURNEY AT HOME
   - Probe the social location of the reader and the reading community:
     General social categories, such as nationality, gender, race, ethnic identity, class and economic status, sexual orientation, and religious affiliation
     Why do these matter in the way you read the text?
   - The spheres of life addressed and the particular issues raised
     Acknowledge assumptions one brings about economic systems, political structures, the composition and role of family, or the importance of communal stability and security.
     Intersection of your journey with the text so that your story becomes part of the story.

- What is going on in the world? *(Columbine, 9/11, suicide bombers, etc.)*
- What is happening in the lives of individual members of the group?
- What is the history of the group?

2. ENCOUNTERING THE BIBLICAL TEXT ⟵ *START HERE*
   - What details "hook" those feelings—specific words, affirmations, questions, characters, situations? What is it about the passage itself or in your own experience that lies behind those feelings?

     WATCH for excess detail!

     Try to imagine how people from other racial, ethnic, economic, or cultural background, or whose life experiences have been different, might read this text.

     What is said in the very specific words of the text one is studying, and also what is assumed or otherwise left unsaid?

   - "Speed bumps" in the text—details that catch your attention and demand closer inspection because they have evoked particularly strong feelings, or because they seem unclear, especially vivid, out of place, or inconsistent.

     Why did I slow down here? What is it about my background that caused this to catch my attention? "Speed bumps" bring you back to #1.

   - Previous experience with the text or its theme:

     Identify what you remember having heard about the passage/its theme in church. How has this text theme been reflected in the popular culture?

     What have you heard in an academic context?

3. CLOSE READING *(Historical criticism)*
   - Translation:

     Prepare your own translation of the passage or read the passage in several modern translations.

     Pay attention to differences in wording and shades of meaning hidden or introduced by the differences in the translation

   - Details of its structure *(Word study—why did the author use this particular word?)*

What verbal clues does the author give about how the various statements or steps of the argument are related to each other?

Make an outline of major (and minor) sections of the passage

4. READING CONTEXTUALLY

- Is all or part of the material also found elsewhere in the Bible?
- The place and function of the passage in the biblical book in which it is found *(e.g., how does Genesis 22 relate to other things we know about Abraham?)*
- The life circumstances of the readers to whom the larger work in which the passage is found was initially addressed
  Earlier embedded contexts
- Relation of the specific passage to what the author is saying about a particular theological agenda
  The particular author's theological voice also has a place in the larger context of the Bible where that voice may find both echoes and dissonances
- In what type of work it is found *(gospel, epistle, myth, narrative)*
  The nature of the book in which the passage you are studying is located
- Locating the specific passage you are studying in the book as a whole
  How does the surrounding material influence what you perceive as the author's principal emphases or concerns?
  What do specific accents or concerns the passage you are studying add to the general agenda of the section of the book in which it is found?
- Get to know that particular community of ancestors-in-the-faith who are the audience of the book one is studying: historical circumstances
  The daily life of the people to whom the book was written
- Theological concerns: author's burning issues or questions; author's faith confession

5. ENGAGING THE TEXT, OTHER READERS, AND OUR COMMUNITIES *(This section brings together the social location of the text and the social location of the reader.)*

- What are the principal issues of the passage?
  What role did they play for the ancient community?
  Are they important issues for you and/or your community?
- What conclusion does the author want you to reach by the end of the passage?
  How would that conclusion have functioned for the author's audience?
  Can you affirm the conclusion *in your time?*
- What is the importance of the passage in your own theology and ministry and in the life of your church?
  What insights does this passage give you about the nature of God, Christ, faith, the gospel, the church, the world, or what it means to be a human being?
  Relationships with other people?

Resource Books Used with the "Celebration of Creation" Retreat

Cameron, Julia. *Blessings: Prayers and Declarations for a Heartful Life*. New York: Tarcher/Putnam, 1998.

——. *Heart Steps: Prayers and Declarations for a Creative Life*. New York: Tarcher/Putnam, 1997.

Fitzgerald, William J. *One Hundred Cranes: Praying with the Chorus of Creation*. Leavenworth, KS: Forest of Peace Publishing, 1996.

——. *Seasons of the Earth and Heart: Becoming Aware of Nature, Self, and Spirit*. Notre Dame, IN: Ave Maria Press, 1991.

Fox, Matthew. *One River, Many Wells: Wisdom Springing from Global Faiths*. New York: Tarcher/Putnam, 2000.

Hamma, Robert M. *Landscapes of the Soul: A Spirituality of Place*. Notre Dame, IN: Ave Maria Press, 1999.

Hanh, Thich Nhat. *Living Buddha, Living Christ*. New York: Riverhead Books, 1995.

Roberts, Elizabeth and Elias Amidon, eds. *Prayers for a Thousand Years: Blessings and Expressions of Hope for the New Millennium*. San Francisco, CA: HarperSanFrancisco, 1999.

Sams, Jamie. *Earth Medicine: Ancestors Ways of Harmony for Many Moons.* San Francisco, CA: HarperSanFrancisco, 1994.

Simsic, Wayne. *Natural Prayer: Encountering God in Nature.* Mystic, CT: Twenty-Third Publications, 1991.

Van Matre, Steve. *The Earth Speaks.* Greenville, WV: Institute for Earth Education, 1983.

Wiederkehr, Macrina. *Seasons of Your Heart.* San Francisco, CA: HarperSanFrancisco, 1991.

Resource Books for the Retreat "Remembering Our Stories"

Albert, Susan Wittig. *Writing from Life: Telling Your Soul's Story.* New York, NY: G. P. Putnam's Sons, 1996.

Ban Breathnach, Sarah. *The Simple Abundance Companion: Following Your Authentic Path to Something More.* New York, NY: Warner Books, Inc., 2000.

Biffle, Christopher. *Garden in the Snowy Mountains: An Inner Journey with Christ as Your Guide.* San Francisco, CA: Harper & Row, Publishers, 1989.

Broyles, Anne. *Journaling: A Spirit Journey.* Nashville, TN: The Upper Room, 1988.

Capacchione, Lucia. *The Creative Journal: The Art of Finding Yourself.* North Hollywood, CA: Newcastle Publishing Co., Inc., 1989.

DeSalva, Louise. *Writing as a Way of Healing: How Telling Our Stories Transforms Our Lives.* San Francisco, CA: HarperSanFrancisco, 1999.

Ealy, C. Diane. *The Woman's Book of Creativity.* Hillsboro, OR: Beyond Words Publishing, Inc., 1995.

Fincher, Susanne F. *Creating Mandalas for Insight, Healing and Self-Expression*. Boston, MA: Shambhala Publications, 1991.

Hagan, Leigh Kay. *Internal Affairs: A Journalkeeping Workbook for Self-Intimacy*. San Francisco, CA: HarperSanFrancisco, 1990.

Hays, Edward. *Prayers for a Planetary Pilgrim: A Personal Manual for Prayer and Ritual*. Easton, KS: Forest of Peace Books, 1988.

Klug, Ronald. *How to Keep a Spiritual Journal: A Guide to Journal Keeping for Inner Growth & Personal Discovery*. Minneapolis, MN: Augsburg Fortress Press, 1993.

Koontz, Christian, R.S.M. *The Living Journal: A Way toward Freedom in the Service of Life*. Kansas City, MO: Sheed & Ward, 1991.

Progoff, Ira. *At a Journal Workshop: The Basic Text and Guide for Using the Intensive Journal Process*. New York, NY: Dialogue House Library, 1975.

Remen, Rachel Naomi. *My Grandfather's Blessings: Stories of Strength, Refuge, and Belonging*. New York, NY: Riverhead Books, 2000.

Rupp, Joyce. *The Cup of Our Life: A Guide for Spiritual Growth*. Notre Dame, IN, 1997.

Sams, Jaime. *Dancing the Dream . . . The Seven Sacred Paths of Human Transformation*. San Francisco, CA: HarperSanFrancisco, 1998.

Solly, Richard, and Roseann Lloyd. *Journey Notes: Writing for Recovery and Spiritual Growth*. New York, NY: Harper & Row Publishers, 1989.

Sullivan, Paula Farrell. *The Mystery of My Story: Autobiographical Writing for Personal and Spiritual Development*. Mahwah, NJ: Paulist Press, 1991.

Wiederkehr, Macrina. *Seasons of Your Heart*. San Francisco, CA: HarperSanFrancisco, 1991.

Retreat Evaluation for "Living as God's Beloved"

Please respond to the following statements to help us plan for future retreats:

1. **I decided to attend this retreat because . . .**
   My roommate talked me into it.
   I love our spiritual life retreats and cannot imagine missing one.
   I heard it would be a great experience.
   I have been struggling with my spiritual life and thought this might help.
   I wanted to get off campus.
   I heard there would be S'MORES!
   I've missed it before and wanted to try it once before I graduate.
   I've been participating in Monmouth Christian Fellowship where I heard a lot about the fall retreat. I've never been on a retreat so I thought I'd try it.
   I wanted some time to just be.
   I need more focus in my prayer life. I thought this might help.
   I heard we were going to make prayer shawls.
   Just needed some time away from classes and stuff.

2. **For me, the most meaningful part of this retreat was . . . Why?**
    The Bible study and discussion Friday night that carried
      through the whole weekend.
    Being with other students I had not met before and getting to
      know them.
    Making prayer shawls and other things that seemed to bring
      out details of the Bible passages we talked about on Friday.
    Food, fun, and games! I loved the fellowship by the fire, too.
    Writing the poem about being Beloved was really cool.
    Getting to do different things. I would never take time at
      school—I don't have the time—to do some of the creative
      art sorts of things we did—and they were fun!
    Making the collage. It was really neat the way all the pieces I
      cut out of the magazines came together—I never imagined
      I could do something like that.
    The late night discussions and fellowship.
    I can't pick a single part—they each had meaning in their own
      way. I really liked everything we did and how it all hung
      together on the theme.
    The Bible studies. Speedbumps are a great approach!
    The prayer shawls!
    Having a safe place to talk about and share brokenness on Sat-
      urday afternoon.

3. **My spirituality was fed by . . .**
    The Bible studies and discussions.
    Singing around the fire.
    The prayers we offered for each other . . .
    The way the theme helped me see how much God works in our
      lives and wants to be involved with us.
    Watching the fire sitting among friends; just being in this place.
    I don't know how to say this—or even if it is ok—but I felt "fed"
      when we did the collages and shawls—it was like my mind
      could wander freely and somehow God kept coming in.
    Being in nature in the winter, a time of year when I usually just
      huddle inside trying to stay warm.
    Listening to the thoughts, ideas, struggles, and successes of
      others—even people of other faiths. You cannot fully know

someone until you know them spiritually, and you know what they believe and trust in.

Getting to do things for other people when I didn't have to— like getting up early on Saturday to make breakfast for everyone else.

Walking in the woods during our free time on Saturday. It's so nice to be away from buildings and concrete.

Thinking about what to put on my prayer shawl and why— and looking for images in the dye. That was amazing!

The Bible studies really sank into my soul because of the art projects.

4. **Additional things that would have fed my spiritual life are . . .**
It was all great—I just want more! Do we have to leave?

More time to share our personal faith stories.

I can't think of anything else.

Maybe an optional early morning devotion each day?

Being with the group that got up early and saw the deer in the woods. I would love to have seen them.

I'm not sure. I haven't processed everything we did yet. I mean, I am still thinking about all we've done together and how we've grown into such a close group. I wouldn't know what else to add.

Maybe a guided meditation.

More personal reflection time or journaling time.

More chocolate!

A prayer partner.

Being outside more—but it was too cold!

More singing.

5. **I would like to have had more . . .**
Time here—I'm not ready to go back.

Sleep.

Alone time.

I can't think of anything—this was all great.

Worship.

More of all of it—I need to find ways to put time like this into my life at the college.

Blankets!
Quiet time.
Ideas for my prayer shawl.
Discussion—I really liked the Bible study discussions.
Same as number 4.
Bacon! But after you explained why we didn't have it this time, it was OK.

6. **The creative arts activities were . . .**
Really cool!
Lots of fun.
A neat way to focus on the scriptures and retreat theme.
Surprising! I didn't think I could do anything arty.
Awesome—especially the prayer shawls. I can't wait to show mine off at school.
Great. The collage will hang in my room reminding me that I am God's beloved!
Relaxing and fun.
So wonderful! They really helped me look at my spiritual life and feel like I was connecting to God in ways I'd never imagined could be.
Great fun and made me think about the Bible passages we read. I never thought I'd learn to write a lament on a retreat!
AWESOME! I am definitely saving magazines so I can do more collages!
Great fun—and stimulating—you know—they made me think.
Fun! I can't believe all the neat stuff I get to take home.

7. **I would attend a retreat like this again.** _12_ Yes   _0_ No
Everyone who submitted an evaluation form (12 of 14 participants) checked yes. The faculty member and I did not fill out evaluation forms.

Retreat Evaluation for "Celebration of Creation"

Please respond to the following statements to help us plan for future retreats:

1. **I decided to attend this retreat because . . .**

    I needed to get away to relax and reflect on my life and where it's going.

    I thought it would be fun and relaxing.

    I had fun in past years on it.

    I wanted to get to know the other Christians at school better. I also wanted to learn more about my relationship with God.

    I wanted to get in touch with God again, and this is perfect for that. I needed a time that has to be just me and God.

    It sounded like fun and I needed to get away.

    I heard about other retreats and wanted to give it a shot.

    Many of my friends were participating and I thought it would be a healthy get-away from school for the mind and soul.

    I desperately needed a *Break*.

    It sounded like fun.

I needed to get away off campus and I wanted to meet new people. I thought how better to do that than actually improve my spiritual life also.

Jimmy Thomas recruited me.

It is an opportunity to step outside of campus life, reflect, relax, and enjoy the company of others. It is a time for rejuvenation and reaffirmation.

I thought it would be fun, and I just love retreats. I heard about it at MCF so I decided to come.

I *loved* the past four [retreats]!

I *needed* to clear my mind and reconnect with God in me.

2. **For me, the most meaningful part of this retreat was . . . Why?**

The first night with the "big rock" story and the description of God story because the biggest problems in life can be solved by putting God first. I needed to be reminded of that.

The free time—it was when we truly got to know each other.

Relaxing and enjoying the people around me.

Having meals and game time together with everyone. I have gotten to know everyone a lot better.

The solitude, silent lunch, and the nature walk because it was a good time to just think and pray and talk with God.

Just hanging out. It was amazing the comfort level between us all.

Taking a step back from school and reflecting on things besides homework, class, and tests.

Meeting new people and sharing in their happiness.

The time spent.

Getting to know people better.

The alone time and forest walk.

Getting to know each person better and feel like we've united as brothers and sisters no matter what faith we call our own.

The free time in which we could relax, play, or talk with others. That is when I felt I could take care of anything I needed to on the retreat.

Just hanging out with everyone late at night. Everyone was themselves and it was just really nice.

The walk—we forget to relax and remember what God made for us.

Connecting with each other and the nature walk on Saturday afternoon. Connecting was meaningful because I received a lot from being in community with those who are like-minded and curious about their own spirituality. The nature walk was meaningful for me because I best connect with God in nature—it's easy to feel how sacred and connected everything is while I'm in nature.

3. **My spirituality was fed by . . .**

Intimate conversations with friends. Their affirmation of my being/purpose was God sending me a message.

Worship.

The natural world and the energy of people around me.

Reflecting on what has been given to me (food, opportunities, etc.) This was especially so during our silent meal time.

Music.

The peace I felt.

Too many things to count. It has been building since I was born.

Others' beliefs and spirit—I found new strength for what I believe. (Also nature!)

The zen walk.

Thinking.

The group activities and conversations I had with other people.

The silence to reflect and remember what we're living and breathing for.

Moments or expansive times of silence that led to contemplation and introspection.

The quiet time in the woods. Just thinking about creation and all of the detail that went into the world.

The community by the fire and conversation.

Collecting leaves and objects from nature to put in my collage.

4. **Additional things that would have fed my spiritual life are . . .**

More of an intimate/discussion centered setup. I was glad when we just sat and talked on Saturday night.

Time by ourselves.
Nothing.
Bible study.
More music. I'm a big fan of the music.
More singing, praise, and worship.
I had plentiful opportunities. I can't think of any others.
More time of reflection and silence or conversation about belief
    and acceptance.
Another week of this!
Bible study/another worship time/we should have all had to go
    off on our own and journal or have a guided devotion.
More time as a group with more activities.
More worship time.
More time for discussion. Suggested topics of discussion: group
    oral reflections on spirituality, spiritual journeys, and per-
    spectives on faith life.
Spending "required" time meditating on scripture.
A longer walk with some pausing for special things to be seen.
More sharing and talking/journaling exercises.

5. **I would like to have had more . . .**
    Same as above.
    Worship.
    Time in general to spend here and enjoy life.
    Lessons about Christianity, Creation, anything.
    Maybe a little sermon or special message (longer than those we
        had) that we can listen to, and also something we could
        open our Holy Books to search through.
    More singing.
    Small group directed discussion.
    Focused conversation.
    Nothing I could think of.
    Small group activities (3–4 people)/ "prayer partners"—get a
        partner and go off and pray together
    Same as above.
    Group time.
    Nothing/everything seemed very well spaced.
    Quiet time/singing

Activities with conversation.
I think I would like to do this kind of thing more in my own
life.

6. **The creative arts activities were . . .**
Very fun and helped me take my mind off problems and put it
into creative mode.
FUN
A lot of fun.
Fun and a great way to spend the day.
Very hard! It was very fun, but maybe not so much next time
because it's definitely something I am not confident in.
Fun, and relaxing too.
Tons of fun and they turned out awesome. I'm definitely going
to put up my ink/string thing in my room!
Awesome and fun.
Awesome!
A lot of fun and very relaxing.
Amazing. I had so much fun and they really helped me to look
deeper into things.
Amazing, stimulating, so fun.
Extremely helpful, challenging, thought provoking, and over
all enjoyable.
Really great. They made me think about things and really look
at things.
AWESOME! I never get to be creative otherwise.
AWESOME! Loved the string project.

7. **I would attend a retreat like this again.** _16_ Yes _0_ No
Everyone who submitted an evaluation form (16 out of 19 students) checked yes. One of the original 20 students who came to
the retreat fell ill and had to leave at 11 a.m. on Saturday.

APPENDIX K

Sample Text for a Retreat Brochure

The title of the retreat should be prominent on your brochure. Also, it is helpful to include a descriptive phrase like "A time set apart to seek God." Include the following:

- a schedule of events
- a list of things participants need to bring
- a description of the retreat site
- registration instructions
- the cost per person (if any)
- whom to contact for additional information
- a general description of the group for whom the retreat is being held—i.e., a local youth group, an intergenerational group from one or more congregations, the students, faculty, and staff from one or more colleges, etc.

WHO SHOULD ATTEND?

(Name of sponsoring institution) spiritual life retreats are for students and faculty of all faiths. The programs are designed to provide participants with an opportunity to experience the gifts of nature, silence, prayer, meditation, discussion, and fellowship in a retreat setting intended to help us focus on our spiritual development and well-being. Wherever you are on your faith journey, you are invited to join others in a weekend of spiritual companionship, seeking renewed awareness of God in your life at college.

WHERE ARE WE GOING?
(Name of Retreat Facility) is a ministry founded by (name of founding organization) in (location) to serve inner-city youth and offer them an affordable summer camp experience. The rest of the year it is available for groups to rent for conferences, training meetings, and retreats. It is located about 25 miles northeast of (our college/our church), and offers dormitory style sleeping space for up to 60 persons in a large lodge. The facility also includes a large meeting room, dining area, several fireplaces, and a fully equipped kitchen.

RETREAT SCHEDULE

FRIDAY, (MONTH/DAY)

4:30 P.M.	Leave from . . .
5:00–5:15	Arrive at (name of retreat site)
5:15–6:00	Move in & Get Out Food!
6:00–7:00	EAT!
7:00–9:00	Session One—brief description or title for the session
9:00–11:00	Community Time: Games, Conversation, etc.
??	Goodnight!

SATURDAY, (MONTH/DAY)

8:00–9:30	Breakfast
9:30	Gathering (this could be a morning devotion, meditation experience, sharing thoughts from their experience the night before, etc.)
10:30–10:30	Session 2—Brief description or title for the session
10:30–Noon	Creative Arts Activity

12:00–12:45	Lunch
12:45–1:00	Gathering Again
1:00–3:00	Session 3—Brief description or title for the session
3:00–5:30	Sacred Space Time (i.e., free time!)
5:30–6:00	Prepare Dinner
6:00–7:00	Dinner
7:00–9:00	Session 4—Brief description or title for the session
9:00–11:00	Community Time: Games, Conversation, etc.

SUNDAY, (MONTH/DAY)

7:30–9:30	Breakfast
9:30–9:45	Session 5—Brief description or title for session
9:45–10:30	Time for closing worship and to reflect together on the weekend
10:30–11:15	Clean-up Camp/Load-up Stuff
11:15	Closing thoughts—give the participants a memento to take home with them, something appropriate to the theme of the weekend—a glass heart, a compass, a lapel pin, etc.
11:30	Leave for Home

STUFF YOU NEED TO BRING!
1. Sleeping bag or bedroll
2. Pillow
3. A favorite poem or short reading
4. Tablet or notebook
5. Pen or pencil
6. Holy book from your faith tradition
7. Your imagination
8. An open mind

OPTIONAL STUFF
1. Board games (Trivial Pursuit, Backgammon, Risk, etc.)
2. Playing cards
3. Your favorite stuffed animal

Interested in going? Contact:
Name of Contact Person
(Contact Person's Title) at (Phone Number Here)
Or drop by the *(indicate location)*
or send an e-mail to *(e-mail address)*.
Pictures of previous retreats are available on the
(sponsor's name) website: *(list URL)*
This event is offered to participants free of charge
(or this event will cost each participant $XX.00)

Notes

Introduction

1. Gerald G. May, M.D., *Will and Spirit: A Contemplative Psychology* (San Francisco: Harper & Row, 1982), 71.

2. Dr. Bruce G. Epperly, *The Spirituality of Campus Ministry*, lecture on January 8, 2003, at Wesley Theological Seminary, Washington, DC.

3. "Much of the drug attraction for the young in our culture comes from their being starved for transcendent experiences in worship, in school, and at home." (Matthew Fox, *Creativity: Where the Divine and the Human Meet* [New York: Tarcher/Putnam, 2002], 227.) "All around us we see the symptoms of our disconnection from Spirit and of our unacknowledged hunger for ecstasy—anorexia and bulimia, depression, violence, drug addiction, and broken marriages . . . we need joy, rapture, and ecstasy in our lives as much as we need physical food." (Jalaja Bonheim, *The Hunger for Ecstasy: Fulfilling the Soul's Need for Passion and Intimacy* [Emmaus, PA: Rodale Books, 2001], 2).

4. Henri J. M. Nouwen, *Life of the Beloved: Spiritual Living in a Secular World* [New York: Crossroad, 1993], 28. "At times we find ourselves stuck in our belief that our interests and our abilities are too small to make a difference for God or to touch another life." (Beverly J. Shamana, *Seeing in the Dark: A Vision of Creativity and Spirituality* [Nashville, TN: Abingdon Press, 2001], 15.)

5. "Human life ceases to be human not when we do not have all the answers but when we no longer have the courage to ask the really important questions." (Daniel L. Migliore, *Faith Seeking Understanding: An*

Introduction to Christian Theology [Grand Rapids, MI: Eerdmans, 1991], 5.)

6. Mary Caroline Richards, *Centering in Pottery, Poetry, and the Person* (Hanover, NH: Wesleyan University Press, 1989), 109.

7. "Because the phenomenon of busy-ness has become so pervasive, contemplative pause is increasingly crowded out of our experience. Mentoring contexts that most profoundly serve the formation of adult faith provide an initiation into the power of pause." (Sharon Daloz Parks, *Big Questions, Worthy Dreams: Mentoring Young Adults in Their Search for Meaning, Purpose, and Faith* [San Francisco, CA: Jossey-Bass, 2000], 145.)

8. "1. A strong or exaggerated sense of masculinity stressing attributes such as physical courage, virility, domination of women, and aggressiveness. 2. An exaggerated sense of strength or toughness." *The American Heritage Dictionary of the English Language, Fourth Edition.* Copyright © 2000 by Houghton Mifflin Company.

9. Marcus J. Borg, *Meeting Jesus Again for the First Time: The Historical Jesus and the Heart of Contemporary Faith* (San Francisco, CA: HarperSanFrancisco, 1994), 87–88. Borg indicates that for Christians secondhand religion "consists of thinking that the Christian life is about believing what the Bible says or what the doctrines of the church say" (88).

10. Translated by Walter Kaufmann and published in New York by Scribner's in 1970 with the title *I and Thou*.

11. Marcus J. Borg, *The God We Never Knew: Beyond Dogmatic Religion to a More Authentic Contemporary Faith* (San Francisco, CA: HarperSanFrancisco, 1987), 42.

12. Borg, *The God We Never Knew*, 42.

Chapter I

1. M. Scott Peck, *The Different Drum: Community Making and Peace* (New York: Simon & Schuster, 1987), 55.

2. Lee G. Bolman and Terrence E. Deal, *Reframing Organizations: Artistry, Choice, and Leadership* (Hoboken, NJ: Jossey-Bass Division of Wiley & Sons, 2003), 402.

3. Kosoke Koyama, "The Hand Painfully Open," *Lexington Theological Quarterly,* April 1987, 22:42.

4. Christianity, of course, is not the only religion with extremist enclaves that profess such outrageous exclusivism as characteristic of the Divine.

5. Stephen G. Post, "The Inadequacy of Selflessness: Divine Suffering and the Theology of Love," *Journal of the American Academy of Religion* (Summer 1988), 56:213.

6. Carol Ochs and Kerry M. Olitzky, *Jewish Spiritual Guidance: Finding Our Way to God* (San Francisco, CA: Jossey-Bass, Inc., 1997), 25.

7. Peck, 101.

8. William C. Placher, *Narratives of a Vulnerable God: Christ, Theology, and Scripture* (Louisville, KY: Westminster John Knox Press, 1984), 55.

9. Peck, 56–57.

10. Coming to understand oneself in relationship to others.

11. Joseph A. DiNoia, *"Christian Universalism: The Nonexclusive Particularity of Salvation in Christ,"* in Carl E. Braaten and Robert W. Jenson, eds. *Either/Or: The Gospel or Neopaganism* (Grand Rapids, MI: Eerdmans, 1995), 44.

12. Post, 224.

13. Robert N. Bellah, et al. *Habits of the Heart: Individualism and Commitment in American Life* (San Francisco, CA: Harper & Row, 1985), 143.

14. Julie A. Gorman, *Community That Is Christian: A Handbook for Small Groups* (Grand Rapids, MI: Baker Books, 2002), 46.

15. Alan Gerwith, *"Common Morality and the Community of Rights"* in Gene Outka and John P. Reeder, Jr., *Prospects for a Common Morality* (Princeton, NJ: Princeton University Press, 1993), 34.

16. Bellah, 84.

17. Bellah, 84.

18. Ellie Maynard Adams, *Religion and Cultural Freedom* (Philadelphia, PA: Temple University Press, 1993), 2.

19. Alasdair MacIntyre, *After Virtue* (Notre Dame, IN: University of Notre Dame Press, 1981), 57.

20. MacIntyre, 115.

21. MacIntyre, 122.

22. Sondra Wheeler, *DM-C141-Moral Discernment in a Context of Pluralism.* Washington, DC: Wesley Theological Seminary, 14 June 2004.

23. Parks, 124.

24. Gerwith, 30.

25. Wheeler, 14 June 2004.

26. Josef Pieper, *The Four Cardinal Virtues* (Notre Dame, IN: Notre Dame Press, 1966), xi.

27. Wheeler, 14 June 2004.

28. Wheeler, 14 June 2004.

29. Wheeler, 14 June 2004.

30. Pieper, 4–5.

31. MacIntyre, 11.

32. Tikua Frymer-Kensky, *"The Image: Religious Anthropology in Judaism and Christianity,"* in Frymer-Kensky, et al., eds. *Christianity in Jewish Terms* (Boulder, CO: Westview Press, 2000), 334.

33. Migliore, 78.

34. Jurgen Moltmann, *God in Creation* (Minneapolis, MN: Fortress Press, 1993), 216.

35. Gerwith, 37.

36. MacIntyre, 122.

37. MacIntyre, 212.

38. MacIntyre, 81.

39. MacIntyre, 59.

40. Peck, 26.

41. Parker J. Palmer, *To Know as We Are Known: Education as a Spiritual Journey* (San Francisco, CA: HarperSanFrancisco, 1993), x.

42. Bellah, 281.

43. MacIntyre, 227.

44. Gorman, 13. Note the current popularity of the television show *Survivor.*

45. Peck, 249–250.

46. Gilbert C. Meilander, *The Theory and Practice of Virtue* (Notre Dame, IN: University of Notre Dame Press, 1984), 4.

47. Rev. John D. McInnis, *Unpublished Sermon* (First Christian Church, Jefferson City, MO: January 3, 1988).

48. *Webster's New World Dictionary of the American Language* (Cleveland and New York: World Publishing Company, 1962), 99.

49. Braaten, 31.

50. Logan, James C., *DM-C112-Theology in a Post-Modern and Pluralist Environment*, Washington, DC: Wesley Theological Seminary, 13 January 2003.

51. Marcus J. Borg, *Meeting Jesus Again for the First Time*, 75.

52. Gorman, 13.

53. Bellah, 46.

54. MacIntyre, 114.

55. Gorman, 43.

56. Gorman, 44.

57. Bellah, 148.

58. Parks, 163.

59. Walter Wink, *The Powers That Be: Theology for a New Millennium* (New York: Galilee-Doubleday, 1989), 29.

60. Initially this sentence began, "The world cannot survive. . . ." In reality, biologist E. O. Wilson of Harvard has stated that the rest of creation would manage quite nicely if human beings ceased to exist (*Keeping the Earth: Religious and Scientific Perspectives on the Environment*, VHS, 28 min. (Cambridge, MA: Union of Concerned Scientists, 1995).

61. Gerwith, 39.

62. *The American Family Association: America's Pro-Family Action Web Site* (Tupelo, MS: American Family Association, 2004); available from www.afa.net/ (accessed 16 August 2004).

63. Bellah, 144.

64. Carlos A. Ball, *"Marriage, Same-Gender Relationships, and Human Needs and Capabilities,"* in Lynn D. Wardle, Mark Strasser, William C. Duncan, and David Orgon Collidge, eds., *Marriage and Same-Sex Unions* (Westport, CT: Praeger, 2004), 137.

65. Gorman, 54.

66. Wheeler, 15 June 2004.

67. Adams, 142.

68. Nouwen, 87.

69. Tex Sample, *Blue-Collar Ministry: Facing Economic and Social Realities of Working People* (Valley Forge, PA: Judson Press, 1993), 23.

70. James Fowler defines *destiny* as that which gives advice ("You are meant to do this.") and *vocation* as that which encourages questions ("What are you called to do?"). (James Fowler, *Becoming Adult, Becoming Christian: Adult Development and Christian Faith* [San Francisco, CA: HarperSanFrancisco, 1984], 143). Parker Palmer points to the further dilemma of not being able to explain oneself to an achievement oriented, winner-take-all culture should one's vocation run counter to culturally dictated values. "Vocation at its deepest level is, 'This is something I can't not do, for reasons I'm unable to explain to anyone else and don't fully understand myself but that are nonetheless compelling.'" (Parker J. Palmer, *Let Your Life Speak: Listening for the Voice of Vocation* [San Francisco, CA: Jossey-Bass, 2000], 25.)

71. Meilander, 75.

72. Carol Geary Schneider and Robert Shoenberg, *Contemporary Understandings of Liberal Education: The Academy in Transition* (Washington, DC: Association of American Colleges and Universities, 1998), 12.

73. Meilander, 72.

74. "There are too few networks of belonging in which young adults are encouraged to reflect critically on the primary images, symbols, and stories-ideologies-myths that shape their souls and their society. A strong empathic, moral imagination—not just on behalf of the self but on behalf of the other as well—is increasingly critical to the practice of citizenship and the vocation of a faithful adulthood in a world marked by social diversity and the awareness of suffering on a global scale" (Parks, 124).

75. Parks, 163.

76. Meilander, 54 and 57.

77. Parker J. Palmer, *To Know as We Are Known*, xiv–xv.

188 Wonder and Other Life Skills

78. MacIntyre, 211.
79. Gorman, 16.
80. Peck, 171.
81. Edmund S. Morgan, ed. *Puritan Political Ideas, 1558–1794* (Indianapolis, IN: Bobbs-Merrill, 1965), 92 as quoted in Peck, 26.
82. Carter Heyward, *Saving Jesus from Those Who Are Right: Rethinking What It Means to Be Christian* (Minneapolis, MN: Fortress Press, 1999), 63.
83. MacIntyre, 245.

Chapter 2

1. Ronald Heifetz, *Leadership without Easy Answers* (Cambridge, MA: Belknap Press of Harvard University Press, 1994), 35.
2. Wilfried Dettling, "Encounter and the Risk of Change: Religious Experience and Christian-Muslim Dialogues," in *Spirituality across Borders*, ed. Philip Endean (Oxford, England: The Way, 2002), 69.
3. Heifetz, 35.
4. Heifetz, 35.
5. Borg, *Meeting Jesus again for the First Time*, 75.
6. Borg, *Meeting Jesus again for the First Time*, 76–77.
7. Bolman and Deal, 240.
8. Luke Timothy Johnson, *The Creed: What Christians Believe and Why It Matters* (New York: Doubleday, 2003), 53.
9. Mihaly Csikszentmihalyi, *Creativity, Flow and the Psychology of Discovery and Invention* (New York: HarperCollins, 1996), 37.
10. Wink, 14–15.
11. Borg, *The God We Never Knew: Beyond Dogmatic Religion to a More Authentic Contemporary Faith* (San Francisco, CA: HarperSanFrancisco, 1992), 19.
12. Parks, 139.
13. William Edelen, *Toward the Mystery* (Boise, ID: Joslyn-Morris, 1980), 62–63.
14. Justo L. Gonzalez, *The Story of Christianity, Volume I, The Early Church to the Dawn of the Reformation* (San Francisco, CA: HarperSanFrancisco, 1984), 254.
15. Heifetz, 254.
16. Heifetz, 236.
17. Heifetz, 235.
18. Parks, 72.
19. Dettling, 68.
20. Heifetz, 22.
21. Parks, 163.

22. Jon C. Dalton, "Career and Calling: Finding a Place for the Spirit in Work and Community," *The Implications of Student Spirituality for Student Affairs Practice* (San Francisco, CA: Jossey-Bass, 2001), 24.

23. Parker J. Palmer, *The Courage to Teach: Exploring the Inner Landscape of a Teacher's Life* (San Francisco, CA: Jossey-Bass, 1998), 56.

24. Earle Coleman reminds us: "Martin Buber has warned that if the I-It orientation 'is one's constant posture, he will not be fully human.'" (Earle J. Coleman, *Creativity and Spirituality: Bonds between Art and Religion* [Albany: State University of New York Press, 1998], 45.)

25. Borg, *The God We Never Knew*, 45–46.

26. Csikszentmihalyi, 36.

27. Csikszentmihalyi, 37.

28. Bolman and Deal, 240, 406; Parks, xii.

29. Bolman and Deal, 329.

30. Bolman and Deal, 240.

31. Bolman and Deal, 240.

32. Donald E. Messer, *Contemporary Images of Christian Ministry* (Nashville, TN: Abingdon Press, 1988), 164.

33. Csikszentmihalyi, 238.

34. Sallie McFague, *Metaphorical Theology: Models of God in Religious Language* (Philadelphia, PA: Fortress Press, 1982), 129.

35. Bolman and Deal, 267.

36. McFague, 31, 36, 38; Gail R. O'Day, "Probing an Inclusive Scripture," *The Christian Century* (July 3–10, 1996): 692.

37. Carl Daw, "An Interview with Carl Daw," *The Hymn* 40 (April, 1989): 28; O'Day, 692.

38. Avery Dulles, *Models of the Church* (Garden City, NY: Doubleday, 1987), 32; Parker J. Palmer, *The Company of Strangers: Christians and the Renewal of America's Public Life* (New York: Crossroads Publishing Company, 1994), 87.

39. McFague, 36; Daniel B. Stevick, *Language in Worship: Reflections on a Crisis* (New York: Seabury Press, 1970), 54.

40. Maria Harris, *Teaching and Religious Imagination* (San Francisco, CA: HarperSanFrancisco, 1987), 13.

41. Randolph Crump Miller, *The Language Gap and God: Religious Language and Christian Education* (Philadelphia, PA: Pilgrim Press, 1970), 4–5.

42. Robert Allen Evans, *Intelligible and Responsible Talk about God* (Leiden, The Netherlands: E. J. Brill, 1973), 112.

43. Letty M. Russell, *Church in the Round: Feminist Interpretation of the Church* (Louisville, KY: Westminster/ John Knox Press, 1993), 13.

44. Richard R. Niebuhr, *Experiential Religion* (New York: HarperCollins, 1972), 91–104.

45. Palmer, *The Company of Strangers*, 63.

46. Bolman and Deal, 242.

47. Ray Hanania, *Arabs and Muslims Killed after September 11th Related Violence*, accessed 1 March 2004; available from www.hanania.com/hatevictims.html; Internet.

48. Malek Chebel, *Symbols of Islam* (Paris: Editions Assouiline, 1997), 123.

49. Chebel, 44.

50. *Star of David*, 2003, accessed 27 January 2004; available from Jewish Virtual Library at www.us-israel.org/jsource/Judaism/star.html.

51. Parks, 141.

52. Paul F. Knitter, *One Earth, Many Religions: Multifaith Dialogue & Global Responsibility* (Maryknoll, NY: Orbis Books, 1996), 28.

53. Chebel, 102.

54. Chebel, 18.

55. Diana Eck, *A New Religious America: How a Christian Country Has Become the World's Most Religiously Diverse Nation* (San Francisco, CA: HarperSanFrancisco, 2002), 298.

56. Wink, 75.

57. Chebel, 123.

58. Bolman and Deal, 242.

59. Parks, 16.

60. Parks, 17.

61. Palmer, *The Courage to Teach*, xv.

62. Daniel O. Aleshire, *Faith Care: Ministering to All God's People through the Ages of Life* (Philadelphia, PA: Westminster Press, 1988), 51.

63. Palmer, *To Know as We Are Known*, xiv.

64. Thomas H. Troeger, "Personal, Cultural, and Theological Influences on the Language of Hymns," *The Hymn* 38 (October, 1987): 8.

65. Palmer, *To Know as We Are Known*, 55.

66. Christian M. Rutishauser, "A Wild Shoot Grafted: How the Encounter with Judaism Can Transform Christianity," in *Spirituality across Borders*, ed. Philip Endean (Oxford, England: The Way, 2002), 23.

67. Parks, 156.

68. Parks, 156.

69. Alyssa N. Bryant, Jeung Yun Choi, and Maiko Yasumo, "Understanding the Religious and Spiritual Dimensions of Students' Lives in the First year of College," *Journal of College Student Development* 44 (Nov.–Dec. 2003): 726.

70. Bruce G. Epperly and Lewis D. Solomon, *Mending the World: Spiritual Hope for Ourselves and Our Planet* (Philadelphia, PA: Innisfree Press, 2002), 13.

71. Ochs and Olitzky, 138.
72. Knitter, 33.

Chapter 3

1. See Shamana and Richards.
2. For example, see Numbers 14:18–19; Psalms 78:38, 86:5, 99:8, 103:8, 106:45; Joel 2:13; Jonah 4:2; Nehemiah 9:17; Daniel 9:9.
3. Chebel, 18.
4. Post, 215.
5. Chebel, 50.
6. Eck, 232.
7. In view of this, I suppose I should not have been surprised at the subsequent reaction from the community about our use of a Wiccan prayer.
8. Adherents.com, "Major Religions of the World Ranked by Number of Adherents," available from www.adherents.com/Religions_By_Adherents.html; Internet; accessed 28 December 2004.
9. Nouwen, 45.
10. How very arrogant of us as Christians to claim adoption as children of Abraham while somehow expecting God to exclude Abraham's other children, Muslims and Jews, because they are not Christian! "The truest appeal to God's promises to Abraham is one that defines Abraham's family in the most inclusive terms, respecting the uniqueness and legitimacy of each of its members." [Harold Washington, "Abraham's Family as a Prototype for Interfaith Dialogue: Judaism, Christianity, and Islam," *Religious Education* 90.02 (Spring, 1985) 299.]
11. Adherents.com, "Major Religions of the World Ranked by Number of Adherents," available from www.adherents.com/Religions_By_Adherents.html; Internet; accessed 5 September 2004.
12. William C. Placher, 18.
13. Heyward, 81.
14. Koyama, 39.
15. Anthony DeMello, *The Way to Love* (New York: Doubleday, 1991), 27.
16. Refer again to 1 Corinthians 1:18: "The cross is foolishness . . ."
17. Hans-Ruedi Weber, *Power: Focus for a Biblical Theology* (Geneva: WCC Publications, 1989), 167.
18. Barbara Brown Taylor, *God in Pain: Teaching Sermons on Suffering* (Nashville, TN: Abingdon Press, 1998), 121.
19. Taylor, 122.
20. Placher, 21.
21. Logan, 16 January 2003.

22. See Joel 2:13–14; Jonah 3:9–10, 4:2; Psalms 10:13, 106:44–45; Jeremiah 18:7–10, 26:3, 13, 19, 42:10; Exodus 32:12–14; Amos 7:3–6; Deuteronomy 32:36; 2 Samuel 24:16; 1 Chronicles 21:15; Judges 2:18; Hosea 11:8.

23. Clinton J. McCann, Jr. "Expository Articles: Exodus 32:1–14," *Interpretation* 44 (3 July 1980): 278.

24. These are words from the hymn *Here I Am, Lord* by Daniel Schutte. Their lingering in my mind is indicative of the staying power of words combined with music.

25. J. Massyngbaerde Ford, *Bonded with the Immortal* (Wilmington, DE: Michael Glazier, 1987), 169.

26. DiNoia, 43.

27. Washington, 294.

28. McCann, 281.

29. Chebel, 48 and 112.

30. William L. Holladay, "Outcasts and Forebears," *The Christian Century* 113.19 (June 5–12, 1996) 613.

31. Logan, 16 January 2003.

32. Translated by Walter Kaufmann and published in New York by Scribner's in 1970 with the title *I and Thou.*

33. Braaten, 113.

34. Carter Heyward calls this "the patriarchal 'god' that we have shaped in our image (and then praised for shaping us in His)" (Heyward, 69).

35. Mark 6:1–6/John 4:43; John 6:41,ff; Matthew 21:23/Mark 11:28; Luke 5:21, 7:49; John 5:18.

36. Dennis Linn, Sheila Fabricant Linn, and Matthew Linn, *Good Goats: Healing Our Image of God* (Mahwah, NY: Paulist Press, 1994), 7.

37. Placher, 55.

38. As this word appeared in my mind, I questioned whether or not it was the word I wanted to use, but I realized I do see this shift in human understanding as a transgression.

39. "I am the way, the truth and the life. No one comes to the Father except through me."

40. *I Am* being the name God gave in Exodus 3 when Moses asked YHWY whom Moses should say had sent him to the Israelites.

41. Braaten, 95.

42. DiNoia, 42.

43. Frederick Buechner, *Listening to Your Life* (San Francisco, CA: HarperSanFrancisco, 1992), 162. Note: the four masculine references to God have been left as is in this quotation to avoid interrupting the flow of its message with changes to inclusive language.

Chapter 4

1. Neil M. Alexander, ed. *The New Interpreter's Bible: Vol. 1* (Nashville, TN: Abingdon Press, 1994), 345.

2. Frymer-Kensky, 331.

3. John H. Westerhoff, III, *Living the Faith Community: The Church That Makes a Difference* (San Francisco, CA: Harper & Row, 1985), 13.

4. Moltmann, 219.

5. Ochs and Olitzky, 39.

6. Abdulaziz A. Sachedina, "Jews, Christians, and Muslims According to the Qur'an," *Greek Orthodox Theological* Review, no. 31 (1986): 106.

7. Seyyed Hossein Nasr, *Knowledge and the Sacred* (New York: State University of New York Press, 1989), 160.

8. Luke Timothy Johnson, *Faith's Freedom: A Classic Spirituality for Contemporary Christians* (Minneapolis, MN: Augsburg Fortress Press, 1990), 59.

9. Ochs and Olitzky, 39.

10. Epperly and Solomon, 60.

11. Bruce C. Birch, Walter Brueggemann, Terrence F. Fretheim, and David L. Petersen, *A Theological Introduction to the Old Testament* (Nashville, TN: Abingdon Press, 1999), 46.

12. Alexander, 349.

13. Sister Ishpryia, "When Shiva Has Blue Eyes," in Philip Endean, ed. *Spirituality across Borders* (Oxford, England: The Way, 2002), 45.

14. Robert Wuthnow, *Creative Spirituality: The Way of the Artist* (Berkeley: University of California Press, 2001), 274.

15. David Hay, "Spirituality versus Individualism: the Challenge of Relational Consciousness," in Jane Erricker, Cathy Ota, and Clive Erricker, eds., *Spiritual Education: Cultural, Religious and Social Differences* (Brighton, England: Sussex Academic Press, 2001), 106.

16. Hay, 108.

17. Epperly and Solomon, 71.

18. Rachel Pollock, *The Power of Ritual* (New York: Dell Publishing Division of Random House, 2000), 24.

19. Pollock, 16.

20. Borg, *The God We Never Knew*, 117.

21. Sue Monk Kidd, *The Secret Life of Bees* (New York: Penguin Books, 2002), 107.

22. Robert M. Hamma, *Landscapes of the Soul: A Spirituality of Place* (Notre Dame, IN: Ave Maria Press, 1999), 38.

23. Ochs and Olitzky, 96.

24. Borg, *The God We Never Knew*, 123.

25. Walter Wink, 186.

26. Joyce Rupp, *The Cup of Our Life: A Guide for Spiritual Growth* (Notre Dame, IN: Ave Maria Press, 1997), 16.

27. Dalton, 18.

28. May, 89.

29. Cathy A. Malchiodi, *The Soul's Palette: Drawing on Art's Transformative Powers for Health and Well-Being* (Boston & London: Shambhala, 2002), x and 7.

30. Moltmann, 311.

31. Carla DeSola, "Liturgical Dance: State of the Art," in Doug Adams and Michael E. Moynahan, S. J., eds., *Postmodern Worship and the Arts* (San Jose, CA: Resource Publications, Inc., 2002), 99.

32. Malchiodi, 172.

33. Wuthnow, 135.

34. Epperly and Solomon, 48.

35. Ashley M. Calhoun, "The Work of Visual Artists in Worship," in E. Byron Anderson, ed. *Worship Matters, Vol. II: A United Methodist Guide to Worship Work* (Nashville, TN: Discipleship Resources, 1999), 81.

36. Nasr, 76.

37. Nasr, 77.

38. Nasr, 77.

39. Nasr, 78.

40. Malchiodi, 172.

41. Sara Webb Phillips, "The Role of Artists in Worship," in E. Byron Anderson, ed. *Worship Matters: A United Methodist Guide to Ways to Worship: Volume 1* (Nashville, TN: Discipleship Resources, 1999), 162.

42. College junior (international student) reflecting on a retreat experience in November 2003 via e-mail June 2004.

43. College sophomore reflecting on retreat experiences in February 2003 and November 2003 via e-mail June 2004.

44. College 2001 graduate reflecting on retreat experiences between February 1998 and February 2001 via e-mail June 2004.

Chapter 5

1. Howard A. Addison, *Show Me Your Way: The Complete Guide to Exploring Interfaith Spiritual Direction* (Woodstock, VT: Skylight Paths Publishing, 2000), 171–172.

2. David Tacey, "Landscapes of Learning Communities" (paper presented at *Dreaming Landscapes*, a global campus ministries conference, Brisbane, Australia, 4 July 2004).

3. Johnson, *Faith's Freedom*, 126.

4. Addison, 67.

5. Addison, 68.

6. Addison, 69.

7. Addison, 70.

8. The plural of *mitzvah*. In the Jewish tradition, the *mitzvoh* are the 613 commandments originating in the Torah or in ancient rabbinic decree. The term is also used to mean righteous acts or good deeds (Ochs and Olitzky, 207).

9. Addison, 71.

10. College senior reflecting on retreat experience in February 2003 via e-mail in June 2004.

11. College sophomore reflecting on retreat experiences in February 2003 and November 2003 via e-mail in June 2004.

12. College junior (international student) reflecting on a retreat experience in November 2003 via e-mail in June 2004.

13. Ursula King, "Landscapes of Faith and Religion" (paper presented at *Dreaming Landscapes*, a global campus ministries conference, Brisbane, Australia, 2 July 2004).

14. Parks, 141.

15. Nasr, 192.

16. The reader is reminded of footnote 74 in chapter 1: "There are too few networks of belonging in which young adults are encouraged to reflect critically on the primary images, symbols, and stories-ideologies-myths that shape their souls and their society. A strong empathic, moral imagination—not just on behalf of the self but on behalf of the other as well—is increasingly critical to the practice of citizenship and the vocation of a faithful adulthood in a world marked by social diversity and the awareness of suffering on a global scale" (Parks, 124).

Chapter 6

1. Henri J. M. Nouwen, *Life of the Beloved: Spiritual Living in a Secular World*. (New York: Crossroad Publishing, 1993).

2. Nouwen, 26.

3. See the "Roadmap for Biblical Interpretation," in Appendix F.

4. Eugene H. Peterson, *The Message: The Bible in Contemporary Language* (NavPress Publishing Group, 2002).

5. Available from local crafts supply store or on-line at www.craftsetc .com/Store/Category.aspx?c=1057.

6. Denise Dombkowski Hopkins, *Journey through the Psalms* (St. Louis, MO: Chalice Press, 2002), 110.

7. Hopkins, 111.

8. Hopkins, 77.

9. Hopkins, 82.

10. David Haas, *You Are Mine: The Best of David Haas, Volume 2* (Chicago, IL: GIA Publications, 1995).

11. These are available relatively inexpensively from numerous religious supply companies.

12. Matthew Fox, *One River, Many Wells: Wisdom Springing from Global Faiths* (New York: Tarcher/Putnam, 2000).

13. Note: This activity is not my creation. I learned of it in 1997 through an e-mail forward which has long since been lost in cyberspace. I can pinpoint the year I received it because I used this same activity on a retreat with my students in February, 1998.

14. See Malchiodi, 92–93.

15. I think it is crucial for retreat leaders to participate in the "chores" of the retreat as part of the process of creating community.

Chapter 7

1. The reader is reminded of the quotation from Marcus Borg in chapter 2: "Visions happen, enlightenment experiences happen, paranormal experiences happen. These experiences suggest that reality is far more mysterious than any and all of our domestications—whether scientific or religious—make it out to be. They suggest that reality is more, much more, than modernity has imagined" (Borg, *The God We Never Knew*, 45–46).

2. David Haas, *You Are Mine: The Best of David Haas, Volume 2* (Chicago, IL: GIA Publications, 1995).

3. Susan Wittig Albert, *Writing from Life: Telling Your Soul's Story* (New York, NY: G. P. Putnam's Sons, 1996), ix.

4. B. Kathleen Fannin, *In Search of the River: A Spiritual Journal in Scripture and Verse* (Lima, OH: Fairway Press, 1992), 13.

5. Haas, 9.

6. Haas, notes for song 9 on the CD jacket.

7. This is a detail I remember from a course at the University of Texas at Austin that I took in 1966, *Indians of the Plains* with Dr. J. Gilbert McAllister.

8. Albert, 219.

Chapter 8

1. Malchiodi, 62.

2. Acts 5:15: "As a result, people brought the sick into the streets and laid them on beds and mats so that at least Peter's shadow might fall on some of them as he passed by."

3. This activity was developed by art therapist Evelyn Virshup in 1979 and discussed in Cathy Malchiodi's work on the transformative powers of art for health and well-being (see Malchiodi, 92–93).
4. Malchiodi, 164.
5. Malchiodi, 179.

Chapter 9

1. Robert DeBard, "Millennials Coming to College," in *New Directions for Student Services* (Wiley Periodicals, Inc., no. 106, Summer 2004), 37.
2. DeBard, 38.
3. Hoyt L. Hickman, "The Basic Pattern of Worship," in E. Byron Anderson, ed., *Worship Matters: A United Methodist Guide to Ways to Worship, Volume 1* (Nashville, TN: Discipleship Resources, 1999), 35.
4. Malchiodi, x.
5. Tom Beaudoin, *Virtual Faith: The Irreverent Spiritual Quest of Generation X* (San Francisco, CA: Jossey-Bass Publishers, 1998), 160.

Appendix

1. Source: Denise Dombkowski Hopkins, *DM-C-121: Education for Stability and Change* (Washington, DC: Wesley Theological Seminary, June 2003).
2. Frederick Tiffany and Sharon Ringe, *Biblical Interpretation: A Roadmap.* (Nashville, TN: Abingdon Press, 1996).
3. Denise Dombkowski Hopkins, *Education for Stability & Change*, Washington, DC: Wesley Theological Seminary, June 2003. Notes added for myself are in italics.

Works Cited

Adams, Ellie Maynard. *Religion and Cultural Freedom*. Philadelphia: Temple University Press, 1993.

Addison, Howard A. *Show Me Your Way: The Complete Guide to Exploring Interfaith Spiritual Direction*. Woodstock, VT: Skylight Paths Publishing, 2000.

Adherents.com. "Major Religions of the World Ranked by Number of Adherents," available from www.adherents.com/Religions_By_Adherents.html; Internet.

Albert, Susan Wittig. *Writing from Life: Telling Your Soul's Story*. New York: G. P. Putnam's Sons, 1996.

Aleshire, Daniel O. *Faith Care: Ministering to All God's People through the Ages of Life*. Philadelphia: The Westminster Press, 1988.

Alexander, Neil M., ed. *The New Interpreter's Bible: Vol. 1*. Nashville, TN: Abingdon Press, 1994.

The American Family Association: America's Pro-Family Action Web Site. Tupelo, MS: The American Family Association, 2004; available from www.afa.net/; Internet.

Anderson, E. Byron. *Worship Matters, Vol. II: A United Methodist Guide to Worship Work*. Nashville, TN: Discipleship Resources, 1999.

Ball, Carlos A. "Marriage, Same-Gender Relationships, and Human Needs and Capabilities" in Lynn D. Wardle, Mark Strasser, William C. Duncan, and David Orgon Collidge, eds. *Marriage and Same-Sex Unions*. Westport, CT: Praeger, 2004.

Beaudoin, Tom. *Virtual Faith: The Irreverent Spiritual Quest of Generation X*. San Francisco: Jossey-Bass Publishers, 1998.

Bellah, Robert N., et al. *Habits of the Heart: Individualism and Commitment in American Life*. San Francisco: Harper & Row, 1985.

Birch, Bruce C., Walter Brueggemann, Terrence F. Fretheim, and David L. Petersen. *A Theological Introduction to the Old Testament*. Nashville, TN: Abingdon Press, 1999.

Bolman, Lee G. and Terrence E. Deal. *Reframing Organizations: Artistry, Choice, and Leadership*. Hoboken, NJ: Jossey-Bass Division of Wiley & Sons, 2003.

Bonheim, Jujala. *The Hunger for Ecstasy: Fulfilling the Soul's Need for Passion and Intimacy*. Emmaus, PA: Rodale Books, 2001.

Borg, Marcus J. *Meeting Jesus Again for the First Time: The Historical Jesus and the Heart of Contemporary Faith*. San Francisco: HarperSanFrancisco, 1994.

———. *The God We Never Knew: Beyond Dogmatic Religion to a More Authentic Contemporary Faith*. San Francisco: HarperSanFrancisco, 1997.

Braaten, Carl E. *No Other Gospel: Christianity among the World's Religions*. Minneapolis, MN: Fortress Press, 1992.

Bryant, Alyssa N., Jeung Yun Choi, and Maiko Yasumo. "Understanding the Religious and Spiritual Dimensions of Students' Lives in the First Year of College," *Journal of College Student Development* 44 (Nov.–Dec. 2003): 723–45.

Buechner, Frederick. *Listening to Your Life*. HarperSanFrancisco, 1992.

Calhoun, Ashley M. "The Work of Visual Artists in Worship," in E. Byron Anderson, ed. *Worship Matters, Vol. II: A United Methodist Guide to Worship Work*. Nashville, TN: Discipleship Resources, 1999: 76–81.

Chebel, Malek. *Symbols of Islam*. Paris, France: Editions Assouiline, 1997.

Coleman, Earle J. *Creativity and Spirituality: Bonds between Art and Religion*. Albany, NY: State University of New York Press, 1998.

Csikszentmihalyi, Mihaly. *Creativity, Flow and the Psychology of Discovery and Invention*. New York: HarperCollins, 1996.

Daw, Carl. "An Interview with Carl Daw," *The Hymn* 40 (April, 1989): 24–29.

Dalton, Jon C. "Career and Calling: Finding a Place for the Spirit in Work and Community," in *The Implications of Student Spirituality for Student Affairs Practice*. Jossey-Bass, 2001: 17–26.

DeBard, Robert. "Millennials Coming to College" in *New Directions for Student Services*. Wiley Periodicals, Inc., no. 106, Summer 2004: 33–45.

DeMello, Anthony. *The Way to Love*. New York: Doubleday, 1991.

DeSola, Carla. "Liturgical Dance: State of the Art" in Doug Adams and Michael E. Moynahan, S. J., eds. *Postmodern Worship and the Arts*. San Jose, CA: Resource Publications, Inc., 2002: 95–102.

Dettling, Wilfred. "Encounter and the Risk of Change: Religious Experience and Christian-Muslim Dialogue" in Philip Endean, ed., *Spirituality across Borders*. Oxford, England: The Way, 2002, 67–74.

DiNoia, Joseph A. "Christian Universalism: The Nonexclusive Particularity of Salvation in Christ," in Carl E. Braaten and Robert W. Jenson, eds., *Either/Or: The Gospel or Neopaganism*. Grand Rapids, MI: Eerdmans, 1995, 37–48.

Dulles, Avery. *Models of the Church*. Garden City, NJ: Doubleday, 1987.

Eck, Diana. *A New Religious America: How a Christian Country Has Become the World's Most Religiously Diverse Nation*. San Francisco: HarperSanFrancisco, 2002.

Edelen, William. *Toward the Mystery*. Boise, ID: Joslyn-Morris, 1980.

Endean, Philip, ed. *Spirituality across Borders*. Oxford, England: The Way, 2002.

Epperly, Rev. Bruce G., and Rabbi Lewis D. Solomon. *Mending the World: Spiritual Hope for Ourselves and Our Planet*. Philadelphia: Innisfree Press, 2002.

Erricker, Jane, Cathy Ota, and Clive Erricker, eds. *Spiritual Education: Cultural, Religious and Social Differences*. Brighton, England: Sussex Academic Press, 2001.

Evans, Robert Allen. *Intelligible and Responsible Talk about God*. Lieden, Netherlands: E. J. Brill, 1973.

Fannin, B. Kathleen. *In Search of the River: A Spiritual Journal in Scripture and Verse*. Lima, OH: Fairway Press, 1992.

Fox, Matthew. *Creativity: Where the Divine and Human Meet*. New York: Tarcher Putnam, 2002.

Fowler, James. *Becoming Adult, Becoming Christian: Adult Development and Christian Faith*. San Francisco: HarperSanFrancisco, 1984.

Frymer-Kensky, Tikua. "The Image: Religious Anthropology in Judaism and Christianity" in Frymer-Kensky, et al., eds., *Christianity in Jewish Terms*. Boulder, CO: Westview Press, 2000.

Gerwith, Alan. "Common Morality and the Community of Rights" in Gene Outka and John P. Reeder, Jr., *Prospects for a Common Morality*. Princeton, NJ: Princeton University Press, 1993.

Gonzalez, Justo L. *The Story of Christianity, Vol. I: The Early Church to the Dawn of the Reformation*. San Francisco: HarperSanFrancisco, 1984.

Gorman, Julie A. *Community that Is Christian: A Handbook for Small Groups*. Grand Rapids, MI: Baker Books, 2002.

Haas, David. *You Are Mine: The Best of David Haas, Volume 2*. Chicago: GIA Publications, Inc., 1995.

Hamma, Robert M. *Landscapes of the Soul: A Spirituality of Place*. Notre Dame, IN: Ave Maria Press, 1999.

Hanania, Ray. "Arabs and Muslims killed after September 11th–related violence," available from www.hanania.com/hate-victims.html; Internet.

Harris, Maria. *Teaching and Religious Imagination: An Essay in the Theology of Teaching*. San Francisco: HarperSanFrancisco, 1987.

Hay, David. "Spirituality versus Individualism: the Challenge of Relational Consciousness" in June Erricker, Cathy Ota, and Clive Erricer, eds. *Spiritual Education: Cultural, Religious, and Social Differences*. Brighton, England: Sussex Academic Press, 2001, 105–17.

Heifetz, Ronald. *Leadership without Easy Answers*. Cambridge, MA: The Belknap Press of Harvard University Press, 1994.

Heyward, Carter. *Saving Jesus from Those Who Are Right: Rethinking What It Means to Be Christian*. Minneapolis: Fortress Press, 1999.

Hickman, Hoyt L. "The Basic Pattern of Worship" in E. Byron Anderson, ed., *Worship Matters: A United Methodist Guide to Ways to Worship, Volume 1*. Nashville, TN: Discipleship Resources, 1999: 30–36.

Holladay, William L. "Outcasts and Forebears," *The Christian Century* 113.19:613, June 5–12, 1996.

Hopkins, Denise Dombkowski. *DM-C121: Education for Stability and Change*. Washington, DC: Wesley Theological Seminary, 16-20 June 2003.

Hopkins, Denise Dombkowski. *Journey through the Psalms*. St. Louis, MO: Chalice Press, 2002.

Ishpryia, Sister. "When Shiva Has Blue Eyes" in Philip Endean, ed. *Spirituality across Borders*. Oxford, England: The Way, 2002: 42–53.

Johnson, Luke Timothy. *The Creed: What Christians Believe and Why It Matters*. New York: Doubleday, 2003.

———. *Faith's Freedom: A Classic Spirituality for Contemporary Christians*. Minneapolis. MN: Augsburg Fortress Press, 1990.

Keeping the Earth: Religious and Scientific Perspectives on the Environment, VHS, 28 min. Cambridge, MA: Union of Concerned Scientists, 1995.

Kidd, Sue Monk. *The Secret Life of Bees*. New York: Penguin Books, 2002.

King, Ursula. "Landscapes of Faith and Religion." Unpublished paper. "Dreaming Landscapes: A Global Campus Ministries Conference," Brisbane, Australia: July 1–7, 2004.

Knitter, Paul E. *No Other Name? A Critical Survey of Christian Attitudes toward the World Religions*. Maryknoll, NY: Orbis Books, 1985.

Koyama, Kosoke. "The Hand Painfully Open," *Lexington Theological Quarterly* 22:33–43, April 1987.

Linn, Dennis, Sheila Fabricant Linn, and Matthew Linn. *Good Goats: Healing Our Image of God*. Mahwah, NY: Paulist Press, 1994.

Logan, James C. *DM-C112-Theology in a Post-Modern and Pluralist Environment*. Washington, DC: Wesley Theological Seminary, January 13–17, 2003.

MacIntyre, Alasdair. *After Virtue*. Notre Dame, IN: University of Notre Dame Press, 1981.

Malchiodi, Cathy A. *The Soul's Palette: Drawing on Art's Transformative Powers for Health and Well-Being.* Boston & London: Shambhala, 2002.

Massyngbaerde, Ford J. *Bonded with the Immortal.* Wilmington, DE: Michael Glazier, 1987.

May, Gerald G. *Will and Spirit.* San Francisco: Harper & Row, 1982.

McCann, Clinton J., Jr. "Expository Articles: Exodus 32:1–14," *Interpretation* 44:275–281, July 3, 1980.

McFague, Sallie. *Metaphorical Theology: Models of God in Religious Language.* Philadelphia: Fortress Press, 1982.

McInnis, Rev. John D. "Unpublished Sermon." First Christian Church, Jefferson City, MO, January 3, 1988.

Meilander, Gilbert C. *The Theory and Practice of Virtue.* Notre Dame, IN: University of Notre Dame Press, 1984.

Messer, Donald E. *Contemporary Images of Christian Ministry.* Nashville: Abingdon Press, 1988.

Migliore, Daniel L. *Faith Seeking Understanding: An Introduction To Christian Theology.* Grand Rapids, MI: William B. Eerdmans, 1991.

Miller, Randolph Crump. *The Language Gap and God: Religious Language and Christian Education.* Philadelphia: Pilgrim Press, 1970.

Moltmann, Jurgen. *God in Creation.* Minneapolis, MN: Fortress Press, 1993.

Nasr, Seyyed Hossein. *Knowledge and the Sacred.* New York: State University of New York Press, 1989.

Niebuhr, Richard R. *Experiential Religion.* New York: HarperCollins, 1972.

Nouwen, Henri J. M. *Life of the Beloved: Spiritual Living in a Secular World.* New York: Crossroad Publishing, 1993.

Ochs, Carol and Kerry M. Olitzky. *Jewish Spiritual Guidance: Finding Our Way to God.* San Francisco: Jossey-Bass, Inc., 1997.

O'Day, Gail R. "Probing An Inclusive Scripture," *The Christian Century:* July 3–10, 1996, 692–94.

Palmer, Parker J. *Let Your Life Speak: Listening for the Voice of Vocation.* San Francisco: Jossey-Bass, 2000.

———. *The Company of Strangers: Christians and the Renewal of America's Public Life.* New York: The Crossroads Publishing Company, 1994.

———. *The Courage to Teach: Exploring the Inner Landscape of a Teacher's Life.* San Francisco: Jossey-Bass, 1998.

———. *To Know as We Are Known: Education as a Spiritual Journey.* San Francisco: HarperSanFrancisco, 1993.

Parks, Sharon Daloz. *Big Questions; Worthy Dreams: Mentoring Young Adults in Their Search for Meaning, Purpose, and Faith.* San Francisco: Jossey-Bass, 2000.

Peck, M. Scott. *The Different Drum: Community Making and Peace.* New York: Simon & Schuster, 1987.

Peterson, Eugene H. *The Message: The Bible in Contemporary Language.* NavPress Publishing Group, 2000.

Phillips, Sara Webb. "The Role of Arts in Worship" in E. Byron Anderson, ed. *WorshipMatters, Vol. I: A United Methodist Guide to Ways to Worship.* Nashville, TN: Discipleship Resources, 1999.

Pieper, Josef. *The Four Cardinal Virtues.* Notre Dame, IN: Notre Dame Press, 1966.

Placher, William C. *Narratives of a Vulnerable God: Christ, Theology, and Scripture.* Louisville, KY: Westminster John Knox Press, 1984.

Post, Stephen G. "The Inadequacy of Selflessness: Divine Suffering and the Theory of Love," *Journal of The American Academy of Religion* 56:213–28, Summer 1998.

Richards, M. C. *Centering in Pottery, Poetry, and the Person.* Hanover, NH: Wesleyan University Press, 1989.

Rupp, Joyce. *The Cup of Our Life: A Guide for Spiritual Growth.* Notre Dame, IN: Ave Maria Press, 1997.

Russell, Letty M. *Church in the Round.* Louisville, KY: Westminster/John Knox Press, 1993.

Rutishauser, Christian M. "A Wild Shoot Grafted: How the Encounter with Judasim Can Transform Christianity" in Philip Endean, ed. *Spirituality across Borders.* Oxford, England: The Way, 2002, 18–30.

Sachedina, Abdulaziz A. "Jews, Christians, and Muslims According to the Qur'an," *Greek Orthodox Theological* Review, no. 31 (1986)

Sample, Tex. *Blue-Collar Ministry: Facing Economic and Social Realities of Working People.* Valley Forge: Judson Press, 1993.

Schneider, Carol Geary and Robert Shoenberg. *Contemporary Understandings of Liberal Education: The Academy in Transition.* Washington, DC: Association of American Colleges and Universities, 1998.

Shamana, Beverly. *Seeing in the Dark: A Vision of Creativity and Spirituality.* Nashville, TN: Abingdon Press, 2001.

"Star of David;" available from www.us-israel.org/jsource/Judaism/star.html; Internet: Jewish Virtual Library.

Stevick, Daniel B. *Language in Worship: Reflections on a Crisis.* New York: The Seabury Press, 1970.

Tacey, David. "Landscapes of Learning Communities." Unpublished paper. *Dreaming Landscapes: A Global Campus Ministries Conference*, Brisbane, Australia, July 1–7, 2004.

Taylor, Barbara Brown. *God in Pain: Teaching Sermons on Suffering.* Nashville: Abingdon Press, 1998.

Troeger, Thomas H. "Personal, Cultural, and Theological Influences on the Language of Hymns and Worship," *The Hymn* 38 (October, 1987):7–16.

Washington, Harold. "Abraham's Family as a Prototype for Interfaith Dialogue: Judaism, Christianity, and Islam." *Religious Education* 90.02 (Spring 1995):286–301.

Weber, Hans-Ruedi. *Power: Focus for a Biblical Theology.* Geneva: WCC Publications, 1989.

Webster's New World Dictionary of the American Language. Cleveland, OH, and New York: The World Publishing Company, 1962.

Westerhoff, John H. *Living the Faith Community: The Church that Makes a Difference.* San Francisco: Harper & Row, 1985.

Wheeler, Sondra. *DM-C141- Moral Discernment in a Context of Pluralism.* Washington, DC: Wesley Theological Seminary, June 2004, 14–18.

Wiederkehr, Macrina, *Seasons of Your Heart.* HarperSanFrancisco, 1991.

Wink, Walter. *The Powers that Be: Theology for a New Millennium.* New York: Galilee-Doubleday, 1989.

Wuthnow, Robert. *Creative Spirituality: The Way of the Artist.* Berkeley: University of California Press, 2001

Other Works Consulted

Ban Breathnach, Sarah. *The Simple Abundance Companion: Following Your Authentic Path to Something More.* New York: Warner Books, Inc., 2000.

Barth, Karl. "The Revelation of God as the Abolition of Religion." In *Christianity and Other Religions*, John Hick and Brian Hebblewaite, eds.. Philadelphia: Fortress Press, 1980, 32–51.

Berryman, Jerome W. "The Nonverbal Nature of Spirituality and Religious Language," in Jane Erricker, Cathy Ota, and Clive Erricker, eds., *Spiritual Education: Cultural, Religious and Social Differences.* Brighton, England: Sussex Academic Press, 2001, 8–21.

Biffle, Christopher. *Garden in the Snowy Mountains: An Inner Journey with Christ as Your Guide.* San Francisco: Harper & Row, Publishers, 1989.

Bisschops, Ralph, and James Francis, eds. *Metaphor, Canon and Community: Jewish, Christian and Islamic Approaches.* New York: Peter Lang, 1999.

Boulding, Maria. *The Coming of God.* Collegeville, MN: The Liturgical Press, 1982.

Bradshaw, Tim. "Grace and Mercy: Protestant Approaches to Religious Pluralism" in Andrew D. Clark and Bruce W. Winter, eds. Grand Rapids, MI: Baker Book House, 1992, 227–36.

Broyles, Anne. *Journaling: A Spirit Journey.* Nashville, TN: The Upper Room, 1988.

Buttrick, David G. "The Nature of Language for Worship," in *The Complete Library of Christian Worship, Vol. IV: Music and the Arts in Christian Worship*, ed. Robert E. Webber. Nashville: Star-Song Publishing Group, 1994, 800.

Cameron, Julia. *Blessings: Prayers and Declarations for a Heartful Life.* New York: Tarcher/Putnam, 1998.

———. *Heart Steps: Prayers and Declarations for a Creative Life.* New York: Tarcher/Putnam, 1997.

———. *The Artist's Way: A Spiritual Path to Higher Creativity.* New York: Tarcher/Putnam, 1992.

Capacchione, Lucia. *The Creative Journal: The Art of Finding Yourself.* North Hollywood, CA: Newcastle Publishing Co., Inc., 1989.

Card, Michael. *Scribbling in the Sand: Christ and Creativity*. Downers Grove, IL: InterVarsity Press, 2002.

Cousar, Charles B. *A Theology of the Cross: The Death of Jesus in the Pauline Letters*. Minneapolis, MN: Fortress Press, 1990.

Crossan, John Dominic. *The Dark Interval: Towards a Theology of Story*. Sonoma, CA: Polebridge Press, 1988.

DeSalva, Louise. *Writing as a Way of Healing: How Telling Our Stories Transforms Our Lives*. San Francisco: HarperSanFrancisco, 1999.

Dozeman, Thomas B. "The Wilderness and Salvation History in the Hagar Story." *Journal of Biblical Literature* 117.01 (1998): 23–43.

Ealy, C. Diane. *The Woman's Book of Creativity*. Hillsboro, OR: Beyond Words Publishing, Inc., 1995.

Fincher, Susanne, F. *Creating Mandalas for Insight, Healing and Self-Expression*. Boston: Shambhala Publications, 1991.

Fitzgerald, William J. *One Hundred Cranes: Praying with the Chorus of Creation*. Leavenworth, KS: Forest of Peace Publishing, 1996.

————. *Seasons of the Earth and Heart: Becoming Aware of Nature, Self, and Spirit*. Notre Dame, IN: Ave Maria Press, 1991.

Foster, Richard J. *Celebration of Discipline: The Path To Spiritual Growth*. San Francisco: Harper & Row, 1988.

Fretheim, Terrence E. "The Repentance of God: A Key to Evaluating Old Testament God-Talk," *Horizons in Biblical Theology* 10:47–70, June 1988.

Fretheim, Terrence E., "Suffering God and Sovereign God in Exodus: A Collision of Images," *Horizons in Biblical Theology* 11:31–56, December 1989.

Gelpi, Donald L., S. J., ed. *Beyond Individualism: Toward a Retrieval of Moral Discourse in America*. Notre Dame, IN: University of Notre Dame Press, 1989.

Hagan, Leigh Kay. *Internal Affairs: A Journalkeeping Workbook for Self-Intimacy*. San Francisco: HarperSanFrancisco, 1990.

Hanh, Thich Nhat. *Living Buddha, Living Christ*. New York: Riverhead Books, 1995.

Harris, Elizabeth J. "The Beginning of Something Being Broken: The Cost of Crossing Spiritual Boundaries," in Philip Endean, ed.

Spirituality Across Borders. Oxford, England: The Way, 2002, 6–17.

Hays, Edward. *Prayers for a Planetary Pilgrim: A Personal Manual for Prayer and Ritual*. Easton, KS: Forest of Peace Books, 1988.

Johnson, Luke Timothy. *Religious Experience in Earliest Christianity*. Minneapolis, MN: Fortress Press, 1998.

Joy, Donald M. *Bonding: Relationships in the Image of God*. Waco, TX: Word Books, 1985.

Klug, Ronald. *How to Keep a Spiritual Journal: A Guide to Journal Keeping for Inner Growth and Personal Discovery*. Minneapolis, MN: Augsburg Fortress Press, 1993.

Koontz, Christian. R.S.M., *The Living Journal: A Way Toward Freedom in the Service of Life*. Kansas City, MO: Sheed & Ward, 1991.

Kuam, Kristen E., Linda S. Schering, and Valarie H. Ziegler. *Eve & Adam: Jewish, Christian and Muslim Readings on Genesis and Gender*. Indianapolis, IN: Indiana University Press, 1999.

Lester, Toby. "What Is the Koran?" *The Atlantic Monthly* (January 1999): 43–56.

Lindbeck, George. *The Nature of Doctrine: Religion and Theology in a Postliberal Age*. Philadelphia: Westminster Press, 1984.

McWilliams, Warren. *The Passion of God: Divine Suffering in Contemporary Protestant Theology*. Macon, GA: Mercer University Press, 1985.

Miller, Vachel W., and Merle M. Ryan, eds. *Transforming Campus Life: Reflections on Spirituality and Religious Pluralism*. New York: Peter Lang, 2001.

Nesbitt, Eleanor. "Religious Nurture and Young People's Spirituality: Reflections on Research at the University of Warwick," in June Erricker, Cathy Ota, and Clive Erricer, eds. *SpiritualEducation: Cultural, Religious, and Social Differences*. Brighton, England: Sussex Academic Press, 2001, 130–42.

Neville, Robert Cummings, ed. *Ultimate Realities: A Volume in the Comparative Religious Ideas Project*. Albany, NY: State University of New York Press, 2001.

Nikaido, S. "Hagar and Ishmael as Literary Figures: An Intertextual Study" *Vetus Testamentum* 51.02 (2001):219–42.

Pollock, Rachel. *The Power of Ritual*. New York: Dell Publishing Division of Random House, 2000.

Progoff, Ira. *At A Journal Workshop: The Basic Text and Guide for Using the Intensive Journal Process.* New York: Dialogue House Library, 1975.

Raitt, Thomas M. "Why Does God Forgive?" *Biblical Theology* 13:38–58, June 1991.

Race, Alan. *Interfaith Encounter: The Twin Tracks of Theology and Dialogue.* London: SCM Press, 2001.

Rahner, Karl. "Christianity and the Non-Christian Religions." In *Christianity and Other Religions.* John Hick and Brian Hebblewaite, eds. Philadelphia: Fortress Press, 1980, 52–79.

Reinhartz, Adele. "Reflections on Table Fellowship and Community Identity," *Semia* 86.01: 227–33.

Remen, Rachel Naomi. *My Grandfather's Blessings: Stories of Strength, Refuge, and Belonging.* New York: Riverhead Books, 2000.

Roberts, Elizabeth and Elias Amidon, eds. *Prayers for a Thousand Years: Blessings and Expressions of Hope for the New Millennium.* San Francisco: HarperSanFrancisco, 1999.

Rodd, Cyril S. "The Promise of Redemption," *The Expository Times* 99:18–19, October 1987.

Sams, Jaime. *Dancing the Dream . . . The Seven Sacred Paths of Human Transformation.* San Francisco: HarperSanFrancisco, 1998.

Sams, Jamie. *Earth Medicine: Ancestors Ways of Harmony for Many Moons.* San Francisco: HarperSanFrancisco, 1994.

Sarot, Marcel. "Suffering of Christ, Suffering of God?" *Theology* 95:113–19, March–April 1992.

Scriven, Tal. *Wrongness, Wisdom, and Wilderness: Toward a Libertarian Theory of Ethics and the Environment.* New York: State University of New York Press, 1997.

Simsic, Wayne. *Natural Prayer: Encountering God in Nature.* Mystic, CT: Twenty-Third Publications, 1991.

Solly, Richard, and Roseann Lloyd. *Journey Notes: Writing for Recovery and Spiritual Growth.* New York: Harper & Row, Publishers, 1989.

Spufford, Margaret. "The Reality of Suffering and the Love of God," *Theology* 88:441–46, November 1985.

Steinberg, Milton. *Basic Judaism*. Orlando, FL: Harcourt Brace & Company, 1975.

Straub, Gail. *The Rhythm of Compassion: Caring for Self, Connecting with Society*. Boston: Tuttle Publishing, 2000.

Sullivan, Paula Farrell. *The Mystery of My Story: Autobiographical Writing for Personal and Spiritual Development*. Mahwah, NJ: Paulist Press, 1991.

Troeltsch, Ernst. "The Place of Christianity Among the World Religions," in *Christianity and Other Religions*, John Hick and Brian Hebblewaite, eds. Philadelphia: Fortress Press, 1980, 11–31.

Van Matre, Steve. *The Earth Speaks*. Greenville, WV: The Institute for Earth Education, 1983.

Westley, Richard. *Redemptive Intimacy*. Mystic, CT: Twenty-Third Publications, 1981.

Wright, Andrew. *Spirituality and Education*. New York: Routledge/Falmer, 2000.

Index